Kathy Schrock's
Every Day of the School Year Series

Endangered Species:
Activities for Understanding the Process of Extinction

Roberta Solomon Endich

A Publication of Linworth Learning

Linworth Publishing, Inc.
Worthington, Ohio

Library of Congress Cataloging-in-Publication Data

Endich, Roberta Solomon.
    Endangered species / Roberta Solomon Endich.
        p. cm. – (Linworth learning)
    Includes bibliographical references (p.).
    ISBN 1-58683-071-6 (perfect bound)
        1. Endangered species—Study and teaching (Elementary)—Activity programs. I. Title.
    II. Series.

QL83.15 .E56 2002
372.3'5—dc21   2001058347

Published by Linworth Publishing, Inc.
480 East Wilson Bridge Road, Suite L
Worthington, Ohio 43085

1-58683-071-6

5 4 3 2

✦ Table of Contents ✦

❖ Table of Contents ❖

Table of Contents

❖ About the Author ❖

oberta Solomon Endich is a library media specialist at the M. E. Small Elementary School in West Yarmouth Massachusetts, on Cape Cod. Living in an area where many species are currently on the Red List, Ms. Endich has a personal interest in endangered animals. The Red List of Threatened Species is published by the IUCN (International Union for Conservation of Nature and Natural Resources). It provides taxonomic conservation status and distribution information on taxa, and is designed to determine the relative risk of global extinction. They are listed as Critically Endangered, Endangered and Vulnerable.

She is a graduate of Kean University in New Jersey and received her M.Ed. in library media studies from Bridgewater State College in Massachusetts. She began her teaching career in the 1970s, teaching high school English in New Jersey, and then left the teaching profession for the allure of Cape Cod and a stint at operating her own retail business. Having returned to teaching, Ms. Endich lives on Cape Cod with her two children and their dogs, Rainbow and Sunshine.

A Word From Kathy Schrock

Welcome to the Every Day of the School Year Series! As an educator, library media specialist, and now technology administrator, I know how important it is for the classroom teacher to extend the learning experiences in the classroom. With the current focus on standards-based teaching, learning, and assessment, I felt it was important to supply classroom teachers and library media specialists with activities that directly support the curriculum, but at the same time, allow for creative teachers to provide supplementary and extension activities for their students.

The activities in this series are varied in scope, but all of them provide practical tips, tricks, ideas, activities, and units. Many of the activities include related print and Internet sites that are easily collected by the classroom teacher before engaging in the activity. There are handouts, worksheets, and much more throughout the books, too.

In my job as technology administrator for a school district, I am often able to plan lessons with teachers and visit classrooms to observe the teaching of the lesson. In addition, as the creator and maintainer, since 1995, of Kathy Schrock's Guide for Educators <http://discovery school.com/schrockguide/>, a portal of categorized Web sites for teachers, I often receive e-mail from teachers who are searching for practical, creative, and easy-to-implement activities for the classroom. I hope this series provides just the impetus for you to stretch and enhance your textbook, lesson, and standards-based unit by use of these activities!

If you have any titles you would like to see added to the series, or would like to author yourself, drop me a note at *kathy@kathyschrock.net*.

❖ How to Use this Book ❖

In order to preserve the delicate balance of our ecosystems, students need to learn about and understand the process of extinction. Humans share the planet with millions of other species. We are all interrelated in some way. Some of these species are on their way to becoming extinct. Before a species becomes extinct, it becomes threatened and then endangered. If we become aware of the species that are threatened or endangered we can, perhaps, prevent them from becoming extinct.

This book provides cross-curricular, standards-based activities and unit plans for classroom teachers of grades K—5 to help their students engage in an active exploration of endangered species. Species become extinct from both natural and human causes. The process of extinction depends on the extent of the danger to that species. By raising student awareness of this critical issue and providing them with information about conservation efforts and organizations that are dedicated to saving and preserving the world's most endangered wildlife and plant life, we can empower them to make a difference in the future of our planet.

The lessons assist in the development of the ability to inquire scientifically. For the younger grades, the activities are geared to observation and simple explanation and comparison of facts. In the upper grade activities, students will have opportunities to explore, measure, classify, and reflect on the facts they discover. Lessons are grouped thematically with vocabulary activities appearing in several related sections.

Each lesson includes a description of the suggested activity, including preparation, procedure, and evaluation. It also includes grade level recommendations, subjects covered, and related print and Internet resources. There are templates for game activities that incorporate the data students collect in a fun and exciting way, and art activities that delight their sense of creativity and amuse them while they learn.

Curriculum areas covered include life science, social studies, geography, language arts, information literacy, and technology. Resources include a variety of reference materials. There are thousands of authoritative Web sites on endangered species. The recommended selections come from a variety of sources that are grade and age appropriate. Students can learn about researching sites on the Internet, develop note-taking skills, and incorporate the use of word processing, presentation, and data base programs. Included in the Web Resources is a list of teacher sites that offer opportunities to create games for the classroom with free online software. These games can help complete the learning experience.

Select the activities that are appropriate for your grade level and lesson plans. Take into consideration the time limitations, availability of resources and equipment, and proximity to field trip suggestions for your class. There is something of value here for every elementary classroom in pursuit of discovering ways to understand and prevent the destruction of some of our most precious natural resources. The activities in this book align with the following national standards:

How to Use this Book

- McREL's K-12 Compendium of Standards: <http://www.mcrel.org/standards-benchmarks/>
  Refer to page viii for a chart listing each McREL standard and the activities that relate to each standard.

- The American Association of School Librarian's *Information Power II* Information Literacy Standards: <http://www.ala.org/aasl/ip_nine.html> Standards 1,2,3,6,8 and 9.

- ISTE's National Educational Technology Standards (NETS) for Students: <http://cnets.iste.org/> Standards 1,3,4 and 5

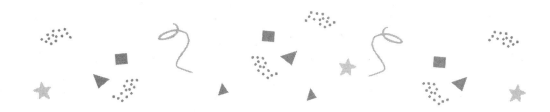

McREL Standards–
❖ Related Activities ❖

McREL Standard	Activity Number
Arts: Art Connections—1	28, 29, 30, 46, 47, 48, 49, 50, 53, 56, 61, 62, 72, 85, 86, 87, 88, 89, 90, 91
Civics—2	57, 58, 59, 64, 65, 66, 67, 70, 71, 72, 73, 74, 75, 76, 77, 78, 79, 84, 104, 105, 106, 107
Geography—1	13, 35, 36, 37, 38, 46, 47, 49, 50, 54, 55, 57, 58, 59, 62, 64, 65, 66, 68, 69
Geography—2	15, 35, 36, 37, 38, 46, 47, 49, 50, 54, 55, 57, 58, 59, 62, 64, 65, 66, 68, 69, 70, 71, 72, 76, 74, 75, 76
Geography—3	35, 36, 37, 38, 39, 40, 41, 42, 43, 44, 45, 46, 47, 49, 50, 54, 55, 57, 58, 59, 62, 64, 65, 66, 68, 69
Geography—4	32, 33, 34, 35, 36, 37, 38, 46, 47, 49, 50, 59, 62, 64, 65, 66, 68, 69, 77, 78, 79, 83, 84, 85, 86, 87, 88, 89, 90, 91
Geography—5	21, 46, 47, 49, 50, 68, 69, 77, 78, 79, 83, 84, 85, 86, 87, 88, 89, 90, 91
Geography—14	9, 10, 13, 15, 43, 44, 45, 46, 47, 49, 50, 54, 55, 57, 58, 68, 69, 70, 71, 72, 73, 74, 75, 76, 77, 78, 79, 83, 84, 104, 105, 106, 107
History: Historical Understanding—1	15, 31, 32, 33, 34, 35, 36, 37, 38, 45, 54, 55, 57, 58, 59, 62, 64, 65, 66, 92, 93, 94, 95, 96, 97, 98, 99, 100, 101, 102, 103, 104, 105, 106, 107
Language Arts—1	2, 3, 4, 5, 7, 31, 32, 33, 46, 47, 49, 50, 51, 52, 60, 61, 77, 78, 79, 81, 82, 83, 84
Language Arts—3	8, 14, 19, 20, 22, 23, 24, 25, 26, 27, 31, 32, 33, 37, 46, 47, 49, 50, 51, 52, 54, 57, 58, 59, 60, 61, 62, 64, 65, 66, 77, 78, 79, 81, 82, 83, 84, 87, 88, 89, 90, 91
Language Arts—4	19, 20
Language Arts—7	8, 9, 10, 14, 18, 22, 23, 24, 25, 26, 27, 29, 30, 31, 32, 33, 46, 47, 49, 50, 51, 52, 60, 61, 77, 78, 79
Life Skills: Life Work—2	22, 23, 24, 25, 26, 27, 60, 61, 104, 105, 106, 107
Life Skills: Thinking and Reasoning—3	1, 11, 12, 13, 16, 17, 22, 23, 24, 25, 26, 27, 39, 40, 41, 46, 47, 49, 50, 51, 52, 60, 61, 70, 71, 72, 73, 74, 75, 76, 79, 81, 82, 83, 84, 92, 93, 94, 95, 94, 97, 98, 99, 100, 101, 102, 103, 104, 105, 106, 107

McREL Standards-
Related Activities

McREL Standard	Activity Number
Life Skills: Thinking and Reasoning—5	13, 19, 20, 22, 23, 24, 25, 26, 27, 51, 52, 60, 61, 79, 81, 82, 83, 84, 92, 93, 94, 95, 94, 97, 98, 99, 100, 101, 102, 103, 104, 105, 106, 107
Life Skills: Working With Others—1	16, 17, 18, 19, 20, 25, 26, 27, 28, 29, 30, 31, 85, 86, 104, 105, 106, 107
Science: Life Science—5	36, 37, 38, 51, 52, 54, 55, 57, 58, 59, 62, 64, 65, 66, 68, 69, 77, 78, 79, 82, 83, 84
Science: Life Science—6	6, 7, 8, 9, 10, 11, 12, 14, 15, 16, 17, 18, 21, 22, 23, 24, 25, 26, 27, 28, 29, 30, 31, 32, 33, 34, 35, 36, 37, 38, 46, 47, 49, 50, 51, 52, 54, 55, 57, 58, 59, 62, 64, 65, 66, 68, 69, 70, 71, 72, 73, 74, 75, 76, 77, 78, 79, 81, 82, 83, 84, 85, 86, 87, 88, 89, 90, 91, 92, 93, 94, 95, 96, 97, 98, 99, 100, 101, 102, 103, 104, 105, 106, 107
Science: Life Science—7	1, 11, 12, 13, 14, 15, 16, 17, 18, 21, 22, 23, 24, 25, 26, 27, 28, 29, 30, 31, 32, 33, 34, 35, 36, 37, 38, 39, 40, 41, 42, 43, 44, 45, 46, 47, 49, 50, 51, 52, 54, 55, 56, 57, 58, 59, 62, 64, 65, 66, 68, 69, 77, 78, 79, 81, 82, 83, 84
Science: Nature of Science—12	16, 17, 52, 60, 61, 64, 65, 66, 68, 69, 70, 71, 76, 92, 93, 94, 95, 96, 97, 98, 99, 100, 101, 102, 103
Technology—2	23, 24, 25, 26, 27, 50, 81, 82, 83, 84
Technology—4	3, 4, 23, 24, 25, 26, 27, 50

Activities

Activity 1:

Classroom Collection and Preparation

Subjects: Life science, geography, art, technology and social studies

Grade levels: 1, 2, 3, 4, and 5

> The classroom teacher and students will collect necessary materials for the Endangered Animal unit.

Preparation:

- Read the Endangered Species Act of 1973, available from the U.S. Fish and Wildlife Service Web site.
- Collect print materials for students to use in art projects, such as magazines and posters.
- Decide which animals you will include in your units. You may have to limit the number, type or location, or make it a class decision.

Related Internet Resources:

U.S. Fish and Wildlife Service. *The Endangered Species Act and What We Do*. Update 16 February 2001.
6 August 2001.
<http://endangered.fws.gov/whatwedo.html#General>

Ongoing Vocabulary Activities:

These activities will provide multiple methods for the entire class and individual students to record their endangered species vocabulary words.

Creating a Vocabulary Journal

Subject: Language arts
Grade levels: 1 and 2 (3, 4, and 5)

This activity is intended to help students who do not have access to or cannot use a computerized database to keep their vocabulary words and definitions in order.

Preparation:

Assemble dictionaries and notebooks for each student.

Procedure:

- Give each student a small notebook in which to keep an Endangered Animal Vocabulary Glossary.
- As classroom activities proceed, have students enter new words that they encounter.
- Have them look up unfamiliar words in the dictionary, record the definitions, and share their words and definitions on a weekly basis.
- Students may decorate their notebooks with a picture of an endangered species.

Evaluation:

Students will be able to build their own Endangered Animal glossaries.

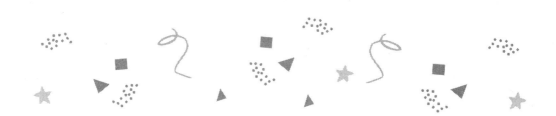

Creating an Individual Computer Glossary

Subjects: Language arts, technology
Grade levels: 4, 5

This activity will employ a database program, such as Microsoft Access, to maintain a personal alphabetized vocabulary list for each student.

Preparation:

■ Familiarize students with the database software.

■ The entire class should enter extinct, endangered, threatened, and species. The rest may vary as individual knowledge develops.

Procedure:

■ As the Endangered Species unit develops, students will journal new words that they need to define.

■ Students will enter these words into a database that they can access for future reference.

Evaluation:

Students will be able to enter their vocabulary words into a database program and sort them alphabetically.

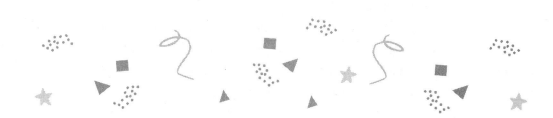

Creating a Class Glossary

Preparation:

■ Familiarize students with the database software.

■ Students should know how to merge databases.

■ At the end of the unit, students merge their individual databases to create a class glossary.

Word Wall for Endangered Species

Subject: Language arts

Grade levels: 1, 2, 3, 4, and 5

> Word walls, designed to promote group learning and be shared by a classroom of children, are organized collections of words displayed in large letters on a wall or display area in a classroom.

Preparation:

Choose a location in the classroom and head the section with a card that reads "Endangered Species Words." Cut oak tag strips to 9" x 3."

Procedure:

■ Add new words to the wall after each lesson. Make sure students are selective about the words that go on the wall. Once words are determined,

■ Use a word processing program to type each word in extra-large bold font, such as Comic Sans MS 120 point.

■ Print and cut out the words, glue to the oak tag strips, and laminate.

■ Make sure students practice and recognize words and spell them correctly.

■ Have students use these words and review their meanings frequently.

Evaluation:

Students will become familiar with endangered animals terminology and become proficient at selecting the correct word in oral language and written work.

Activity 6:

Extinct Means Gone Forever

Subject: Life science
Grade levels: 1, 2, 3, 4, and 5

> The extinction of a species is a natural process. It is believed that two-thirds of all animal species that once existed are now extinct. However, as a result of human activity, species are now disappearing at a faster rate than ever before. Some predict that in this century, 100 species will disappear each day. To enable students to grasp the concept of extinction, "gone forever," this first section begins with a review of extinct animals.

Preparation:

You will need
- Materials on extinction and extinct species,
- Whiteboard or paper to track brainstorming, and a
- Dictionary.

Procedure:

- Write the sentence "Extinct means gone forever" on the board or paper.
- Ask, "What do you think this phrase means?"
- Discuss the meaning of *extinct*. Have one student look it up in the dictionary and record the definition.
- Invite students to
  - ▶ Share the names of all the extinct animals they know of,
  - ▶ Explain when they think the animals became extinct,
  - ▶ Define why they think these animals are extinct, and
  - ▶ Record all the answers on the board or paper.

Evaluation:

Students will be able to define the word extinct and name several extinct species.

Related Internet Resources:

Past exhibits at the AMNH Library Gallery. 9 September 2000. 23 August 2001.
<http://nimidi.amnh.org/gallery/exhibitspace.html>

Reilly, David. *The Tragedy of the Dodo.* 6 October 2000. 20 August 2001.
<http://www.educationplanet.com/search/redirect?id=2373&mfcat=/search/Environment/Animals/Extinct_Species/&mfcount=30>

Kasnoff, Craig. *In the Wild Overview.* ©2000. 13 September 2001.
<http://www.bagheera.com/inthewild/ext_background.htm>

Define and Understand the Different Kinds of Extinction

Subjects: Interdisciplinary
Grade levels: 1, 2, 3, 4, and 5

Students determine the possible causes of and differences between types of extinction.

Preparation:

You will need

■ Dictionaries and paper for students to record definitions, a

■ List of extinct animals from previous lesson, and a

■ List of vocabulary words for students to learn, such as the following.

Biological diversity (biodiversity): The variety of living organisms within a species, the variations between families and classes, and the variety of ecosystems, habitats, and interactions of species in the wild.

Mass extinction: Periods of accelerated rates of extinction and loss of biodiversity.

Ecosystem: An integrated group of biological organisms located in a particular type of habitat, and the physical environment in which they live. The ecosystem includes the living organisms, habitat structure, factors such as temperature, wind, elevation, and their interactions.

Geographic range: The area where a species may be found.

Extirpation: The complete removal of a particular type of organism from an area, usually a specified geographic area.

Procedure:

Activity 7: Students look up and enter the words from the vocabulary list in their electronic database or vocabulary journal.

Activity 8: Have students brainstorm the causes of extinction for each species on the list from the previous activity. If the concept is too difficult, limit the discussion to dinosaurs and their extinction.

Evaluation:

Students will learn that extinction is caused by many factors and is of two kinds: mass extinction that has taken tens of thousands of years to occur, caused by climate change, extreme geological activity, huge meteors colliding with the Earth, or other natural factors; and the sixth great extinction episode, precipitated by human activities, which appears to be happening very quickly.

Related Internet Resources:

Kasnoff, Craig. *In The Wild Overview.* ©2000. 13 September 2001.
<http://www.bagheera.com/inthewild/ext_background.htm>

ESBN. *Bagheera Classroom Glossary.* ©2000. 11 August 2001.
<http://www.bagheera.com/inthewild/class_glossary.htm>

Activities 9 and 10:

The Sudden Extinction of the Passenger Pigeon

Subject: Life science

Grade levels: 1, 2, 3, 4, and 5

> The study of the passenger pigeon tells us a sad and amazing story about the extinction of an abundant population over the course of just 80 years.

Preparation:

You will need books about and illustrations of the passenger pigeon.

Procedure:

Activity 9: Tell or read the story of the passenger pigeon. Have students note that the passenger pigeon

- Was the most common vertebrate in North America,
- Existed in flocks of more than a billion birds, and
- Was an easy and tasty target. Hunting competitions were held that required killing a minimum of 30,000 birds.
- By 1914, just a single pigeon, named Martha, lived on in a Cincinnati zoo. When Martha died, the passenger pigeon was gone forever.

Activity 10: With the information, have students discuss

- What would it be like to have over a billion birds flying over an area?
- What caused the passenger pigeon to become extinct?
- Could it have been prevented? Suggest some ways.

Evaluation:

Students will be able to understand that extinction is taking place in their lifetime.

Related Print Resources:

Behm, Barbara J. and Balouet, Jean-Christopher, *Endangered Wildlife, In Peril.* Gareth Stevens, 1994, 32 pp.

Coleman, Graham, The Extinct Species Collection, *Passenger Pigeon.* Gareth Stevens, 1996, 24 pp.

Galan, Mark, *There's Still Time.* National Geographic Society, 1997, 40 pp.

Related Internet Resources:

Shenk, Tony. *The Passenger Pigeon. Gone Forever from the Face of the Earth.* April 2000. 8 September 2001.
<http://www.ris.net/~tony/ppigeon.html>

Chipper Woods Bird Observatory. *The Passenger Pigeon.* ©1997—2001.8 September 2001.

<http://www.wbu.com/chipperwoods/photos/passpigeon.htm>

Education Planet. *The Pigeon Collection.* ©2000. 8 September 2001.
<http://www.educationplanet.com/search/redirect?id=26712&mfcat=/search/Environment/Animals/Birds
_(Wildlife)/Doves_and_Pigeons/&mfcount=15

The American Museum of Natural History. "Passenger Pigeons." 8 September 2001.
<http://www.amnh.org/exhibitions/expeditions/treasure_fossil/Treasures/
Passenger_Pigeons/pigeons.html?dinos>

Mumford, A.W. "The Passenger Pigeon." *The Nutty Birdwatcher.* January 1998. 8 September 2001.
<http://www.birdnature.com/jan1898/passengerpigeon.html>

Why Does a Species Become Extinct?

Subject: Life science
Grade levels: 1, 2, 3, 4, and 5

Students develop an understanding of how a species becomes endangered and how to prevent it from becoming extinct.

Preparation:

■ Tap into prior knowledge from the story of the passenger pigeon.

■ Have materials available on extinction and endangerment.

Procedure:

Activity 11: Have students

■ Discuss which species of animal they would miss the most if it became extinct and

■ Keep track of their choices.

Activity 12: Each student will pick an animal and identify

■ Resources that the animal needs to survive and

■ What would have to happen for that animal to become extinct.

Students may list their criteria on the What Animal Would You Miss the Most? chart (see chart on page 10).

Evaluation:

Students will be able to understand what a species needs to prevent extinction.

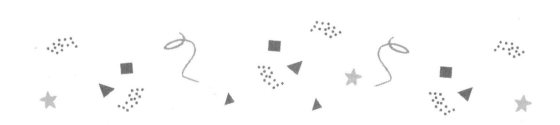

What Animal Would You Miss the Most?

Name of Animal	Resources the Animal Needs for Survival

Activity 13:
What Have We Got to Lose?

Subjects: Critical thinking, life science
Grade levels: 1, 2, 3, 4, and 5

> This activity promotes an understanding of what we might be losing with each species that goes from endangered to extinct.

Preparation:

■ Copy the names of the animals that students listed on their What Animal Would You Miss the Most? charts to the board or chart paper.

■ Have available books on endangered animal species.

Procedure:

■ Ask students

  ► What would be missed if this animal were gone forever?

  ► What benefit does this species offer the world and mankind?

■ Record all answers.

■ Try to expand students' comprehension if they don't understand right away. Some answers might include

  ► Medicines developed through the study of wildlife; prescriptions containing medicines discovered in animals and plants.

  ► Wildlife helps scientists determine quality of the environment.

  ► Species diversity and healthy ecosystems provide food, clean air and water, and fertile soil for agriculture.

  ► Wild animals give humans a sense of vitality.

Evaluation:

Students will be able to identify the value of endangered animals and plants.

Related Internet resource:

Microsoft Corporation. "Endangered Species," Microsoft® Encarta® Online Encyclopedia 2001.
17 August 2001.
<http://encarta.msn.com> © 1997-2000

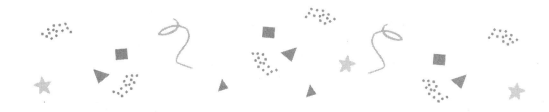

Defining Endangered Species

Subjects: Language arts, life science
Grade levels: 1, 2, 3, 4, and 5

> This activity is designed to help students define and understand the many vocabulary words that deal with endangered species.

Preparation:

- Provide dictionaries and paper or vocabulary journals for students to record definitions.
- Write the words *Endangered, Threatened,* and *Species* on the board or paper.

Procedure:

- Ask students what they think these words mean.
- Talk about the meaning of *endangered*. Have one student look it up in the dictionary and record the definition.
- Talk about the meaning of *threatened*. Have one student look it up in the dictionary and record the definition.
- Talk about the meaning of *species*. Have one student look it up in the dictionary and record the definition.
- Ask students to discuss the differences among *extinct, endangered,* and *threatened*.
- Record all the answers on the board or paper.

Evaluation:

Students will begin to understand that endangered and threatened species are not yet extinct, and what the subtle differences between each term are.

Threats to Species

Subject: Life science
Grade levels: 1, 2, 3, 4, and 5

> Students deepen their understanding of how a species becomes endangered and how to prevent it from becoming extinct.

Preparation:

Have materials available on extinction and endangerment.

Procedure:

Have students discuss possible causes for endangerment and extinction:

- **Hunting:** A major cause of decline and extinction of species like the bison, trumpeter swan, and passenger pigeon. Legal hunting is no longer a major contributor to extinction in North America, though illegal hunting and poaching are still a big problem.

- **Habitat loss:** Loss of a place to live, reproduce, and find food displaces many species and reduces their numbers.

- **Pollution:** Pesticides like DDT once threatened the bald eagle and peregrine falcon. Their food contained DDT from various sources that caused some of the birds to die from the pesticide or to lay thin-shelled eggs that broke easily. DDT was banned in this country in 1972, but many other forms of pollution threaten species today.

- **Dietary needs:** Some species, like the panda, are very picky about what they eat. Because their diet is very special, habitat loss and changes might make their food scarce or nonexistent, greatly increasing their chances for extinction.

- **Nesting needs:** Some birds and animals need special places to have their young. Many North American birds rely on holes in dead, standing trees for nesting and food. Starlings, which were introduced from Europe, compete with native woodpeckers, bluebirds, and chickadees for nesting sites in tree cavities.

- **Space and territory needs:** Wolves and bears need a large space to range and do not like to share this space. As more space is taken for people, crops, domestic animals and recreation, animals lose the space they need.

- **Slow growth and reproduction rate:** Condors lay only one egg every two or three years. Elephants may have only one youngster every five years. Anything that disrupts their lifestyle can be a major setback to the population.

- **Naturally limited populations:** Some species naturally have small populations. Because island animals have limited space, they have nowhere to go if habitat or food is lost. Humans often introduce competing wildlife and predators that make the existing species very vulnerable.

- **Migration:** As birds and animals migrate and rely on varied habitats, their survival becomes more difficult if changes occur. This stresses the existing populations and limits reproductive success.

Evaluation:

Students will be able to understand what causes a species to become extinct.

Classifying Desk Debris I

Subject: Life science
Grade levels: 1, 2, 3, 4, and 5

> This activity introduces the scientific method of classification.

Preparation:

Provide a gallon-size plastic bag for each student.

Procedure:

■ Direct students to empty out all the debris from their desks, including all types of writing utensils, food, candy, gum, wrappers, bookmarks, glasses, coins, and any other junk.

■ Each student fills up his or her clear plastic bag with this desk trash.

■ Divide the class into six teams of equal size and have each team empty their bags and attempt to "sort" out items and group like items together—for example, all the writing tools—then divide this collection into types of writing tools (pencils, crayons, markers, pens). Each subgroup might be divided even further into yellow pencils, decorative pencils, graphite pencils, and colored pencils. The teams continue dividing and subdividing their desk debris until they have exhausted their imaginations.

■ Students then record their findings in the Desk Debris Record (see page 16). Make sure all components are recorded. If students don't need to claim their items immediately, ask them to leave them grouped for the next lesson.

Evaluation:

Students will be able to understand how scientists divide all living things into organized categories.

Classifying Desk Debris II

Preparation:

Display the Desk Debris Records.

Procedure:

■ Invite students to examine other teams' groupings.

■ Allow time for discussion.

■ Brainstorm:

▶ Did each team have similar items?

▶ Did each team divide the groups the same way?

▶ Do you agree with the other teams' groups and subgroups?

▶ If so, why? If not, why not?

■ Briefly explain that this is the way scientists have divided up all living organisms.

Evaluation:

Students will demonstrate classification of disparate objects.

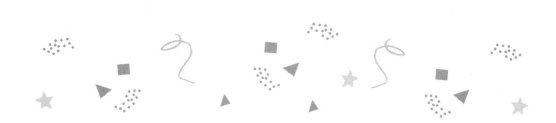

Desk Debris Record

Team Members: _____

_____

Item	Group	Subgroup	Subgroup	Subgroup

Classifying Animals

Subject: Life science
Grade levels: 1, 2, 3, 4, and 5

Students will learn about the five classes of vertebrates: fish, reptiles, amphibians, birds, and mammals, and discuss the invertebrates.

Preparation:

You will need

- A board or chart paper for recording student activity and
- Field guides and other classification books.

Procedure:

- Ask questions: Are fish animals? Are salamanders animals? Are bluebirds animals? Are dogs animals? Are snakes animals?
- Team up the students, and have each team list 20 animals. Be sure to limit the number of mammals (animals with fur).
- From the list have each student group similar animal types and try to come up with a name for each group.

Evaluation:

Students will

- Demonstrate knowledge of the characteristics of the most common animal groups.
- Identify animals within a specific animal group.
- Distinguish between the six most common groups of animals.

Active Research on Classification

Subject: Life science

Grade levels: 1, 2, 3, 4, and 5

This is a self-checking research and brainstorm activity.

Preparation:

You will need

- Materials from previous lessons,
- Internet access, plus
- Encyclopedias, field guides, books, and pamphlets on classification.

Procedure:

- Display the teams' lists of the animal group names.
- Invite students to discuss and explain their methods of grouping.
- Explain the word *taxonomy* and what a taxonomist does.
- Give students an opportunity to compare and correct their groupings with field guides, books, encyclopedias, and the Internet.

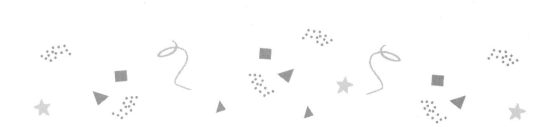

Activity 20:

Learning Classifications

Subject: Life science

Grade levels: 3, 4, and 5

Preparation:

Materials on animal groups

Procedure:

■ Use the groupings the students created in prior activities.

■ Have students discuss their findings on the characteristics of each group of animals.

■ Guide their discoveries by asking them lead questions. Use the following outline.

▶ What are the characteristics of **mammals**? Warm-blooded vertebrate animals of the class Mammalia, including humans, characterized by a covering of hair on the skin and, in the female, milk-producing mammary glands for nourishing the young, who are born alive, except for the small subclass of monotremes.

▶ What are the characteristics of **reptiles**? Cold-blooded, usually egg-laying vertebrates of the class Reptilia, having an external covering of scales or horny plates and breathing by means of lungs. Reptiles include snakes, lizards, crocodiles, turtles, and dinosaurs.

▶ What are the characteristics of **amphibians**? Cold-blooded, smooth-skinned vertebrates of the class Amphibia that characteristically hatch as aquatic larvae with gills. The larvae then transform into adults having air-breathing lungs. Amphibians are capable of living both on land and in water. Frogs, toads, and salamanders are amphibians.

▶ What are the characteristics of **birds**? Any of the class Aves of warm-blooded, egg-laying, feathered vertebrates with forelimbs modified to form wings. Birds range from protected songbirds to species hunted as game and others, such as chickens and turkeys, raised for food.

▶ What are the characteristics of **fish**? Any of numerous cold-blooded aquatic vertebrates of the superclass Pisces, characteristically having fins, gills, and a streamlined body and including specifically

● The class Osteichthyes, having a bony skeleton;

● The class Chondrichthyes, having a cartilaginous skeleton and including the sharks, rays, and skates; and

● The class Agnatha, having round mouths and long, tubelike bodies, and including lampreys and hagfish.

▶ What are the characteristics of **invertebrates**?

● **Sponges** live in water (usually saltwater), are sessile (do not move from place to place), and filter tiny organisms out of the water for food.

● **Coelenterates** have mouths that take in food and get rid of waste and are surrounded by stinging tentacles; jellyfish, corals, and sea anemones.

● **Echinoderms** live in seawater and have external skeletons; starfish, sea urchins, and sea cucumbers.

● **Worms** include flatworms (flukes), roundworms (hookworms), segmented worms (earthworms), and rotifers (philodina).

● **Mollusks** are soft-bodied animals that often live in hard shells. They include snails, slugs, octopi, squid, mussels, oysters, clams, scallops, chitons, and cuttlefish. Mollusks, with 50,000 living species, are the second largest group of invertebrates.

- **Arthropods** are the largest and most diverse of all animal groups. They have segmented bodies supported by a hard external skeleton. Arthropods include insects, arachnids (spiders and their relatives), centipedes, millipedes, and crustaceans like crabs, lobsters, and shrimp.

Evaluation:

Students will begin to recognize familiar classifications and groups of animals.

Related Internet Resources:

"Dictionary.com." ©2001 Lexico LLC. September 10, 2001.
<http://www.dictionary.com>

"Animal Groups." Factmonster.com. ©2000, 2001 Learning Network. September 26, 2001.
<http://infoplease.kids.lycos.com/ipka/A0768513.html>

"Cool Archive: Animals." ©2000—2001 CoolArchive.com. September 26, 2001.
<http://www.coolarchive.com/clipart.cfm?parameter=Animals>

Characteristics of a
Group of Animals

MAMMALS	
REPTILES	
AMPHIBIANS	
FISH	
BIRDS	
INVERTEBRATES	

Select an Animal to Research

Subject: Life science
Grade levels: 1, 2, 3, 4, and 5

These exercises help students identify animal classes by their similar characteristics.

Preparation:

Display the list of animal classes and their characteristics. Put the classifications on the outside of manila envelopes and hang them up separately.

Procedure:

■ List the six classifications of animals from the previous exercise—mammals, reptiles, amphibians, fish, birds, and invertebrates.

■ Have each student

▶ Name an animal he or she would like to learn more about,

▶ Write the animal's name on an index card,

▶ Put his or her name on the back of the card, and

▶ Place it on the display under the correct classification.

▶ Encourage a variety of choices.

Evaluation:

Students will correctly identify the six main animal groups.

Animal Kingdom Graphic Organizer

Subjects: Life science, technology

Grade levels: 4 and 5

Students will create a chart of the divisions of the animal kingdom.

Preparation:

For this activity, students will need to know about taxonomic classification. Have available photographs of animals from each phylum.

Procedure:

Divide the class into groups; each group will work on a separate activity.

Activity 22: Create the headings for the groups on the computer using a word processing program.

Activity 23: Select suitable pictures of a member of each group. Photos can come from magazines or be downloaded from an Internet site and printed.

Activity 24: Arrange the display and put the pieces together.

Evaluation:

Students will graphically demonstrate an understanding of the main taxonomic divisions of the animal kingdom.

Animal Kingdom

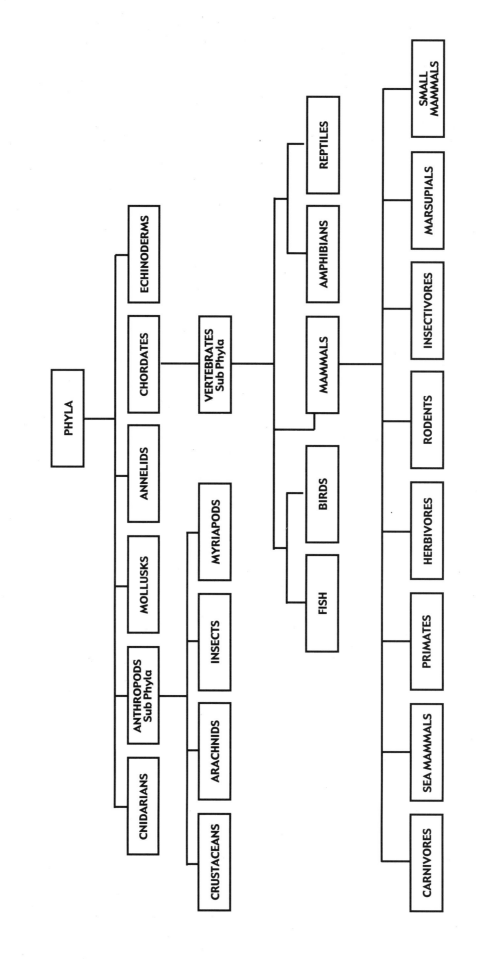

Classification PowerPoint Show

Subjects: Life science, art, and technology
Grade levels: 4 and 5

Students create a hypermedia presentation of the basic animal classifications.

Preparation:

Students will need to be familiar with Microsoft PowerPoint or another presentation software and have access to a computer lab and the Internet.

Procedure:

Activity 25: (Text)

■ Divide students into groups of four and assign each group a class of animals.

■ Each student selects an endangered animal in that class on which to create one introductory slide.

■ The first step is to create the informational content for the slide—the text.

Activity 26: (Graphics) In addition to the text, the slide should include

■ A color photograph downloaded, printed, cut, and pasted from the Internet,

■ The common and scientific name of the animal, and

■ The class it belongs to.

Activity 27: (Combining Slides) Students in each team combine their slides for a simple presentation on their class of animal and present it to the whole class.

Evaluation:

Students will be able to create a simple four-slide show for their group of animals, demonstrating their knowledge of the presentation software and skills specific to that program such as creating, cutting, pasting, editing, and saving.

Creating an Animal Classification Matching Game

Subjects: Life science, art

Grade levels: 1 and 2

Students learn to put animals in their correct classifications.

Preparation:

You will need

■ Card stock;

■ Photos of the various classes: reptiles, mammals, fish, amphibians, insects, and birds; and

■ Large cards with the classes printed on them.

Procedures:

Activity 28:

■ Have students cut out animals that belong to specific animal classes and paste them onto pre-cut card stock.

■ Laminate the cards.

■ Create the written or printed match for the picture cards or let students create them on a word-processing program and glue them on the card stock.

Activity 29: Ask students to

■ Name the animal in the picture and

■ Put animals into their correct groupings.

Evaluation:

Students will create the cards and matches for a Classification Matching Game.

Playing the Animal Classification Matching Game

Subjects: Life science, art
Grade levels: 1 and 2

Students practice putting animals in their correct classifications.

Preparation:

Prepare copies or an overhead of the Classification Matching Game handout.

Procedure:

Students name the animal in the picture and match each animal with its class.

Evaluation:

Students will recognize animal classifications.

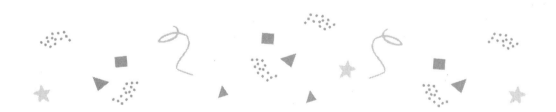

Classification Matching Game

Draw a line connecting the animal picture to the animal word.

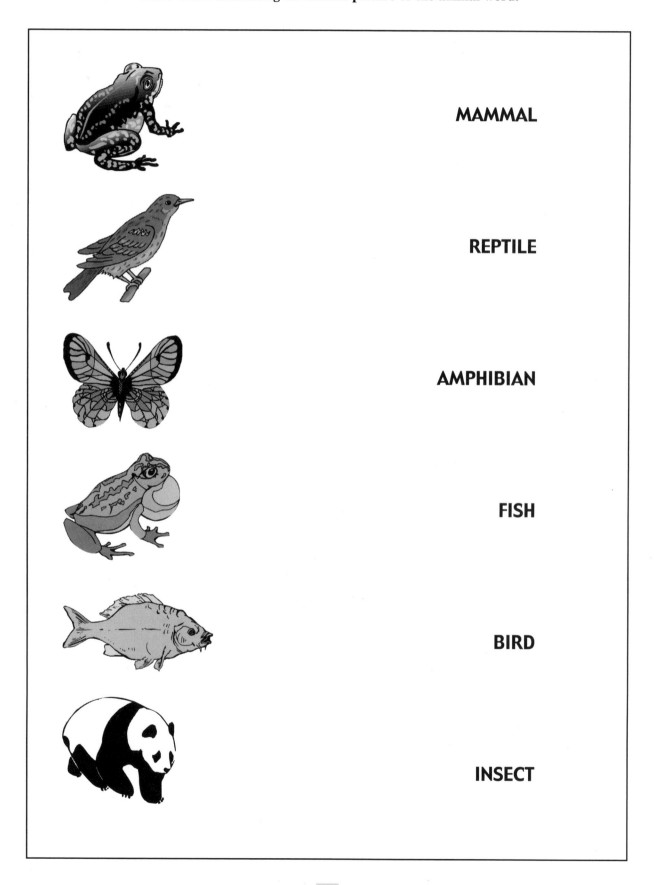

MAMMAL

REPTILE

AMPHIBIAN

FISH

BIRD

INSECT

Activity 31:

Endangered or Not?

Subject: Life science
Grade levels: 1, 2, 3, 4, and 5

Students begin to recognize animals that might be endangered.

Preparation:

Read the Endangered Species Act of 1973, and review and refresh students' knowledge of endangered species.

Procedure:

■ Point out animals the students have selected in prior activities that are endangered.

■ Review the definition of the word *endangered* with the class.

■ Ask students to brainstorm and begin to name endangered species.

■ Challenge them to conjecture why these animals are endangered.

Evaluation:

Students will be able to recognize the criteria for an endangered species.

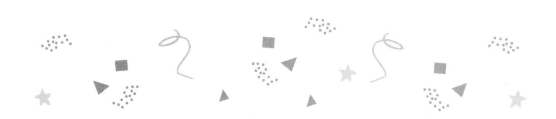

Activities 32 and 33:
Your Personal Habitat

Subject: Life science
Grade levels: 1, 2, 3, 4, and 5

Students learn what a habitat is by relating it to their own and other human habitats.

Preparation:

Have photographs from magazines showing kinds of homes in various parts of the country and the world. If possible, ask students to bring in pictures of their homes. Perhaps they can each borrow the digital camera for a night or buy a disposable camera and then get the house pictures developed.

Procedure:

Activity 32: Discuss the various types of homes your students live in and other types of homes they know about (private home, apartment, trailer, condo). Share pictures.

- How are they different?
- What do all the homes in the class have in common?
- Discuss what types of home someone in another country might have.
- How are they different from ours? Why?
- What do all homes have in common?

Activity 33: Using a Venn diagram, identify the similarities and differences between your personal habitat and the habitat of someone in another country.

Evaluation:

Students will understand what is meant by a habitat.

Personal Habitat Venn Diagram

Name _____

YOUR HOUSE

OTHER HOUSE

BOTH HOUSES

THINGS IN YOUR HOUSE

Activity 34:

Identifying Animal Habitats

Subjects: Life science, geography
Grade levels: 1, 2, 3, 4, and 5

Students list and describe animal habitats.

Preparation:

■ Collect research materials on habitats from the library media center and the Internet.

■ Have on hand whiteboard or paper to track brainstorming.

Procedure:

The habitats are

■ Polar, arctic areas,   ■ Taiga (subarctic evergreen forest),

■ Mountains,   ■ Wetland areas and marshes,

■ Oceans,   ■ Pond,

■ Deserts,   ■ Rivers and lakes,

■ Savannah, grasslands, prairies,   ■ Coral reef,

■ Tropical rainforest,   ■ Deciduous forest,

■ Woodland forest,   ■ Tide pool,

■ Tundra,   ■ Cave.

Using this list,

■ Reintroduce students to the concept of habitats.

■ Have students brainstorm and identify habitats and record their answers.

■ Have them select six or eight familiar ones to work with for other activities.

Evaluation:

Students will understand that Earth supports many different habitats and that each habitat has distinct features.

Related Internet Resources:

Mosbacker, Linda. *Animal Habitats*. ©Art Today. 17 July 2001.
<http://www.uen.org/utahlink/activities/view_activity.cgi?activity_id=3792>

Smithsonian Institution. *Arctic Wildlife Portfolio*. ©1997. 17 July 2001.
<http://www.mnh.si.edu/arctic/html/wildlife.html>

The Evergreen Project. *The Grasslands Biome*. ©1995—1998. 17 July 2001.
<http://mbgnet.mobot.org/sets/grasslnd/animals/index.htm>

Activity 35:

Characteristics of Animal Habitats

Students list and describe the characteristics of animal habitats.

Preparation:

Have on hand whiteboard or paper to track brainstorming.

Procedure:

■ Using the six or eight habitats selected in Activity 34, have students brainstorm and identify features of each.

■ If they are stumped, help them by naming an animal that might live in one.

Evaluation:

Students will demonstrate knowledge of the characteristics of different animal habitats.

Activity 36:

Locating Animal Habitats

Subjects: Life science, geography
Grade levels: 1, 2, 3, 4, and 5

Students locate a habitat on a world map.

Preparation:

This activity builds on students' prior knowledge of the physical description of each habitat. It calls for a large map of the world or globe.

Procedure:

■ List the habitats.

■ Review the characteristics of each with materials from previous lessons.

■ Using the map or globe, encourage students to brainstorm about which habitats exist where and to match a habitat to a place.

Evaluation:

Students will be able to locate a specific habitat on a world map.

Related Internet Resources:

The Franklin Institute. *Neighborhoods*. ©1995—2001 The Franklin Institute Science Museum, 17 August 2001.
<http://sln.fi.edu/tfi/units/life/habitat/habitat.html>

Habitat Word Search and
Word Search Challenge

Subjects: Life science, language arts

Grade levels: 1 and 2 (Activity 37); 3, 4, and 5 (Activity 38)

Students search for hidden words.

Preparation:

Review words from the word wall.

Evaluation:

Students will be able to recognize familiar words about endangered animals.

Habitat Word Search

Name: _____

Find the hidden words.

A	M	Z	F	S	Z	H	C	M	H
R	C	I	A	I	Y	O	W	A	A
C	A	T	Q	L	X	O	L	R	B
T	V	F	O	C	E	A	N	S	I
I	E	D	E	S	E	R	T	H	T
C	C	E	S	A	V	A	N	N	A
M	O	U	N	T	A	I	N	T	T
A	T	S	T	U	N	D	R	A	P

TUNDRA   MARSH
DESERT   MOUNTAIN
CAVE   HABITAT
OCEAN
SAVANNA
ARCTIC

Habitat Word Search Challenge

Name: _____

Find the hidden words.

D	O	D	S	P	A	E	V	U	R	O	K	H	T	U	I	P	Z
L	H	E	A	V	R	L	C	T	R	C	T	T	P	S	A	O	B
H	Q	S	A	B	H	E	L	O	B	I	O	M	E	D	N	N	R
T	B	E	R	U	I	S	D	C	S	K	L	O	L	K	H	D	A
A	T	R	C	G	Y	O	A	A	O	Y	L	J	C	E	P	M	I
A	U	T	T	R	V	D	V	T	R	S	F	L	E	B	J	N
H	H	N	I	O	H	A	V	I	A	O	A	T	H	I	A	C	F
J	A	R	C	Y	O	T	S	G	V	N	R	L	E	R	E	N	O
Z	C	B	Z	L	K	C	U	S	F	E	N	W	R	M	B	P	R
B	V	V	I	V	F	Y	L	N	L	L	R	A	W	E	Y	K	E
P	U	L	Q	T	P	Z	Q	L	D	A	X	S	E	F	E	W	S
H	L	G	N	H	A	C	U	M	W	R	N	X	I	A	O	F	T
G	L	C	J	Y	J	T	S	G	V	H	A	D	T	T	Y	C	Q
G	M	T	O	W	R	G	Y	H	U	Y	F	X	S	X	Y	X	E

BIOME   PREDATOR
RAINFOREST   FOREST
SAVANNA   ECOSYSTEM
OCEAN   HABITAT
BIODIVERSITY   POND
CORALREEF   DESERT
ARCTIC   TUNDRA
GRASSLANDS

Who Lives Here?

Students list and describe animals that live in each habitat.

Preparation:

Have on hand whiteboard or paper to track brainstorming.

Procedure:

- List the six or eight habitats the class selected for investigation in Activity 34.
- List the answers as students brainstorm and name endangered animals that live in each habitat.
- Have students explain why they think a particular animal lives where it does.
- They should then list the characteristics that support that particular animal in that habitat.

Evaluation:

Students will understand why certain animals live where they do.

Related Internet Resources:

Michael, Alex. *Habitat Information.* ©2001. 1 October 2001.
<http://www.cuug.ab.ca:8001/~animal/habitat.html>

Activities 40 and 41:

Locating Animals and Their Habitats

Subjects: Life science, geography
Grade levels: 1, 2, 3, 4, and 5

Students begin to identify the endangered animals in each habitat.

Preparation:

■ Create a Classroom Habitat Display Wall with the names of the six or eight habitats selected by the class printed on large cards. (Follow instructions for Activity 5, page 4.)

■ Have a large map of the world as part of this display.

■ Collect photographs, pictures, and posters of endangered animals for the students to use in their habitat and animal identification and location activities.

Procedure:

Activity 40:

■ List the habitats selected by the class.

■ Ask students to identify an endangered animal and its habitat and to locate the habitat on the map.

Some examples:

■ Deserts—vultures, coyotes, Komodo dragon, great roadrunner, diamondback rattlesnake, scorpion, camel

■ Savanna, grasslands, prairies—African elephant, lion, black-tailed prairie dogs, buffalo, cheetah, Karner blue butterfly

■ Tropical rainforest—golden toad, Smith's dwarf chameleon

■ Woodland, forest—numbat, fat-tailed dwarf lemur, golden lion tamarin

■ Tundra—Arctic wolf, reindeer, Eastern population wolverine

■ Taiga—Siberian tiger, lesser white-fronted goose

■ Wetland areas and marshes—gray bat, Florida panther, wood stork, freshwater mussels, piping plover

■ Pond—Western Pond turtle, Northern leopard frog

■ Rivers and lakes—Coho salmon, Baiji dolphin, river otter

■ Coral reef—Hawaiian green turtle

■ Deciduous forest—gorilla, panda

■ Tide pool

■ Cave

Activity 41: Brainstorming: Animals and Habitats

Have students brainstorm and try to name at least one animal living in each habitat. It is important they understand an animal may live in more than one habitat.

Evaluation:

Students will

- Know the physical description of each habitat,
- Locate an example of the habitat on a world map, and
- Identify animals and plants that live in each habitat.

Related Internet Resources:

The Franklin Institute. Neighborhoods. ©1995—2001, The Franklin Institute Science Museum. 18 August 2001.
<http://sln.fi.edu/tfi/units/life/habitat/habitat.html>

PBS. Great Wall Across the Yangtze. ©1995—2001. 18 August 2001.
<http://www.pbs.org/greatwall/controversy2.html>

Northern Prairie Wildlife Research Center. The Rare Ones. ©Last update 10 October 2001.
<http://www.npwrc.usgs.gov/resource/othrdata/rareone/river.htm>

Rainforest Action Network. Species Extinction; Rainforest Fact Sheet. © 1995—2001. 7 September 2001.
<http://www.ran.org/info_center/factsheets/03b.html>

Woodland Park Zoo. Fat Tailed Wolf Lemur. ©Woodland Park Zoo. Last revision 10 October 2000. 7 September 2001.
<http://www.zoo.org/educate/fact_sheets/night/dlemur.htm> and
<http://www.zoo.org/educate/fact_sheets/day/tamarin.htm>

Kalasinskas, Ron. The Bald Eagle. ©1999—2001 Animals of the Rainforest. 7 September 2001.
<http://www.animalsoftherainforest.org/frames.htm>

Hellenic Ornithological Society. Lesser White Fronted Goose. ©2000. 7 September 2001.
<http://www.ornithologiki.gr/en/oiwnos/i2/ennanox.htm>

What Do You Know About the Rainforests?

Subjects: Life science, geography
Grade levels: 1, 2, 3, 4, and 5

Students begin an exploration of the rainforests. This introduction will reveal what they already know about rainforest habitat.

Preparation:

You will need

- Print material on the rainforest habitat and
- Paper or board to record class answers.

Procedure:

- Ask students
    - ▶ What is a rainforest?
    - ▶ Where are rainforests located?
    - ▶ Why are they so important?
    - ▶ How many animals live in a rainforest?
- Record all answers.
- You may use a KWL chart for this activity to guide students into the next set of activities.

Evaluation:

Students will display their knowledge (assumed and otherwise) of the rainforest. A KWL chart is a table that students fill out during an investigative process. They list what they Know, what they Want to know or find out, and what they Learned during the process.

Whose Life Is in Danger in the Rainforest?

Students identify endangered animals in the rainforest.

Procedure:

Have students, either individually or as a group,

- Investigate rainforest materials,
- Select endangered animal species,
- Collect information on these animals,
- Record information on the Endangered Animals of the Rainforest Habitat handout (page 42), and
- Share the information with the rest of the class.

Evaluation:

Students will be able to identify endangered rainforest animal species and the reasons for their endangerment.

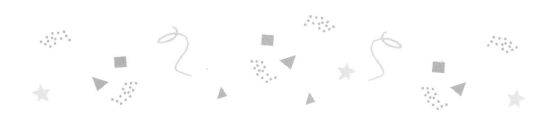

Endangered Animals
of the Rainforest Habitat

Name:_____

Description	Behavior
Color:	Common activities:
Average height:	Diet:
Average weight:	Sleep habits:
Unusual characteristics:	Family life:

Habitat	Lifespan/Endangered Status
Global location(s):	Natural enemies:
Habitat:	Reasons for endangerment:
Migration habits:	Number remaining:

More Facts About Rainforests

Subjects: Life science, technology
Grade levels: 3, 4, and 5

Students use information from Activity 43 to learn more about the rainforest habitats.

Preparation:

Bookmark appropriate rainforest information sites. (This activity requires students to be able to use a browser.)

Procedure:

Ask students to

■ Visit bookmarked Internet sites for information and activities on the rainforest and

■ Share information and resources.

Evaluation:

Students will obtain additional information and share it with the class.

Related Internet Resources:

Raintree Nutrition, Inc. *Rainforest Facts.* ©1996—2001. 2 October 2001.
<http://www.rain-tree.com/facts.htm>

Passport to Knowledge. *Passport to the Rainforest.* ©1998. 2 October 2001.
<http://passporttoknowledge.com/rainforest/intro.html>

Rainforest Conservatory. *Race for the Rainforest.* ©2001 Care2.com, Inc. 2 October 2001.
<http://rainforest.care2.com/

Rainforest Action Network. *Rainforest.org World Rainforest Information Portal.* 2 October 2001.
<http://www.rainforestWeb.org/>

Rainforest Action Network. *Welcome to the Kids Corner.* ©1995—2001. 2 October 2001.
<http://www.ran.org/kids_action/>

Zoom Rainforests. *All About Rainforests.* ©1998—2000 Enchanted Learning. com. 2 October 2001.
<http://www.enchantedlearning.com/subjects/rainforest/>

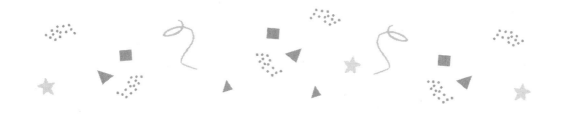

Activity 45:
Who Depends on the Rainforest?

Students make use of available resources to answer the question, "Who depends on the rainforest?"

Preparation:

This activity requires
- Prior knowledge of the rainforest,
- Print materials on the rainforest, and
- Internet access.

Procedure:

Ask students to research answers to these questions:
- How many species live in the rainforest?
- What is the value of rainforest species?
- Where are the major rainforests?
- What are the major threats to rainforests around the world?
- At what rate are we losing rainforests?
- What can we do to protect rainforests?

Evaluation:

Students will comprehend rainforests' potential for our and other species' survival.

Related Internet Resources:

Earth to Kids. *Rainforests*. ©2000 Environmental Defense. 2 October 2001.
<http://www.earth2kids.org/teachers/rainforest.html>

All About Nature, Biomes and Habitats. *A Sampling of Tropical Rainforest Animals*. ©1998—2001 Enchanted Learning. com. 5 October 2001.
<http://www. enchantedlearning.com/subjects/rainforest/animals/Rfbiomeanimals.shtml>

Habitats and Animals

Animal	Habitat	Characteristics

Endangered Animal Biography

Subjects: Life science, language arts, art, geography
Grade levels: 1, 2, 3

Students create an endangered animal report as detailed as their learning level permits.

Preparation:

■ Ask students to select an endangered animal.

■ Guide their choices to include as many of the animal habitats as possible.

■ Create a rubric with the class as to what information will be required to complete the assignment.

Procedure:

These activities may be adapted for either teams or individuals.

Activity 46: Each student or team will complete a biography of an endangered animal and a specific habitat. The report will include where it lives, what it eats, the physical characteristics of the animal and whatever else the class decides.

Activity 47: (Habitat and Location) They will report on the habitat, including climate and global location.

Activity 48: (Picture) Each student will create a picture of the animal with a computer program or draw an illustration of the animal in its habitat.

Activity 49: (Presentation and Display) The class will present and display all these biographies to share.

Evaluation:

Students will be able to match animals to their habitats and describe each.

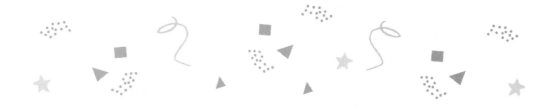

Endangered Animal Database

Subjects: Life science, technology
Grade levels: 4 and 5

Students create a class database for endangered animals.

Prerequisite:

The class is familiar with a computer database program.

Procedure:

■ Ask the class to brainstorm fields appropriate for an endangered animal database. Suggested fields might include name of animal, species, habitat, number left, statistical information (size, weight, eating habits, prey), and whatever else the class decides.

■ Select a student to set up the database form.

■ As each student investigates and obtains information on a designated endangered animal, he or she will enter the information in the database in the correct field. Other students can access this database for information.

Evaluation:

Students will demonstrate their ability to

■ Research and record specific information about endangered animals,

■ Create a database with fields,

■ Enter data into the correct fields, and

■ Query information in a database.

Endangered Animal Reporter

Subjects: Life science, critical thinking
Grade levels: Grades 1, 2, and 3

> Students begin the research process by identifying the type of information they need to gather and where best to obtain it.

Preparation:

Each student selects (or is assigned) an endangered animal to investigate.

Procedure:

- ■ Students will decide and record
    - ▶ What they want to know about their endangered animal and
    - ▶ In what type of library or electronic material they will find the information.
    - ▶ They gather and record their information in the school library or classroom from print and Internet resources.

Evaluation:

Students will demonstrate knowledge of the types of information resources.

Endangered Animal Report

Subject: Life science

Grade levels: 1, 2, and 3

Students use the Endangered Animal Report form to record facts about assigned endangered animals.

Preparation:

You will need

- Print resources on endangered animals,
- Copies of the Endangered Animal Report form for each student, and
- Information from the previous lesson.

Procedure:

Each student will choose another endangered animal and, using the same procedure for Activity 51, locate and record facts about each animal.

Evaluation:

Students will be able to retrieve specific facts about their endangered animal and record the information.

Endangered Animal Report

Type of Animal: _____

Species: _____

Habitat: _____

Geographical Location: _____

How Many Are Left: _____

Eating Habits: _____

Prey: _____

Predators: _____

Why Is This Animal Endangered? _____

_____

_____

_____

_____

Activity 53:
Draw Your Endangered Animal

Subjects: Life science, art

Grade levels: 1, 2, and 3

Using real photographs of their animals, students draw a picture of their endangered species.

Preparation:

You will need

- Photographs of endangered animals and
- Markers, crayons, and pencils

Procedure:

After examining photos of their endangered animal, students will draw a picture of the animal that will become part of a classroom display or an individual report.

Evaluation:

Students will demonstrate their ability to draw an endangered animal.

Draw Your Endangered Animal

This is a picture of a

_____

Activity 54:
Endangered Animal Word Search

Name:_____

Find the hidden words

V	M	A	G	H	J	D	E	Z	P
H	A	N	O	Y	N	O	L	E	A
L	N	T	R	B	I	L	E	B	N
I	A	E	I	A	B	P	P	R	D
O	T	L	L	V	E	H	H	A	A
N	E	O	L	O	A	I	A	I	M
D	E	P	A	X	R	N	N	L	B
I	M	E	C	H	E	E	T	A	H

BEAR   PANDA
ELEPHANT   DOLPHIN
ZEBRA   MANATEE
LION   GORILLA
ANTELOPE   CHEETAH

Endangered Animal
Word Search Challenge

Name:_____

Find the hidden words

R	B	F	Z	C	O	W	Y	W	O	I	J	P	C	M	F	S	R
O	C	P	P	A	J	U	K	I	F	W	A	L	L	A	E	F	H
L	W	P	L	R	W	E	E	L	I	Y	G	A	B	N	R	L	I
L	G	I	E	I	H	T	L	D	U	L	U	T	M	A	R	U	N
E	O	R	M	B	A	H	S	E	R	S	A	Y	F	T	E	Q	O
O	R	M	U	O	L	G	D	B	P	J	R	P	C	E	T	M	C
P	I	S	R	U	E	B	T	E	K	H	Q	U	B	E	D	M	E
A	L	T	K	N	T	I	B	E	F	X	A	S	M	C	Q	Z	R
R	L	Q	O	J	Z	U	L	S	N	E	U	N	X	L	B	Z	O
D	A	Q	O	Z	E	Q	R	T	M	U	X	W	T	L	V	A	S
O	L	H	K	M	N	P	D	T	L	V	M	X	E	H	M	V	T
X	O	G	R	Z	E	B	R	A	L	A	Z	B	T	I	G	E	R
E	O	R	A	N	G	U	T	A	N	E	Y	M	A	D	B	U	Z
K	E	P	A	N	D	A	N	P	T	M	P	A	N	T	H	E	R

BAT	ELEPHANT	ZEBRA	FERRET
PANDA	PLATYPUS	TURTLE	WHALE
TIGER	RHINOCEROS	GORILLA	LEOPARD
LEMUR	WILDEBEEST	PANTHER	CARIBOU
NUMBAT	ORANGUTAN	MANATEE	JAGUAR

Activity 56:
Design a Poster

Subjects: Life science, art
Grade levels: 3, 4, and 5

Students synthesize the information they have collected and create a visual report on an endangered animal.

Preparation:

Assemble materials for posters—poster board, glue, markers, photographs the students can cut and paste.

Procedure:

Ask students to

■ Determine what to include,

■ Gather facts on the endangered animal,

■ Collect the materials they want to use, and

■ Create a poster for classroom display that includes the name, habitat, picture of the animal, and any other information they choose.

Evaluation:

Students will demonstrate their ability to organize their facts visually.

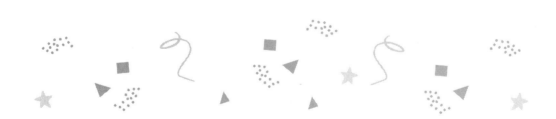

School Newspaper Report

Subjects: Science, language arts

Grade levels: 3, 4, and 5

> This can be a culminating activity for students who have studied one particular animal. They will organize their facts and prepare a news article on that animal for the school or class newsletter.

Procedure:

Activity 57: Discuss the organization and content of a newspaper article:

- First paragraph: Introduce who, what, when, where, and why in a manner that captures readers' attention.
- Middle paragraphs: Provide additional details in an objective manner.
- Final paragraph: Summarize the information.

Activity 58: Examine a well-written newspaper article, determine the important information, and use it as a model for student news articles that include

- A picture of the animal,
- A map showing the location of the species and its habitat, and
- Any vital information on why the animal is endangered and what the reader can do to help it survive.

Evaluation:

Students will be able to create a newspaper article to inform readers about the plight of their particular endangered animal and what might be done to help it.

Related Internet Resources:

Media for Awareness. *Formula for a Well-Written News Article.*
<http://www.media-awareness.ca/eng/med/class/teamedia/newshan2.htm>

Royal British Columbia Museum. *Endangered Species in Endangered Spaces.* ©1995. 19 July 2001.
<http://rbcm1.rbcm.gov.bc.ca/end_species/index_es.html>

Activities 59, 60, and 61

Newsworthy Endangered Animals

Subjects: Life science, language arts

Grade levels: 3, 4, and 5

Students look for news articles on an endangered animal and track this animal for several months, clipping news items and journaling the process.

Preparation:

This activity requires examples of news articles about endangered species plus materials for scrapbooks for each student:

- Two pieces of 9" by 12" oak tag paper
- Colored construction paper
- Hole punch
- Ribbon or rings to bind pages together
- Glue sticks
- Lined writing paper
- Markers and crayons

Procedure:

Activity 59: Tracking Media Coverage

- Introduce students to sample news articles about endangered species.
- Read and discuss the information in each and discuss why the animal is newsworthy.
- Explain that they will be following the same species of animal for a period of time.

Activity 60: Creating a Scrapbook

- Students look for news articles on endangered species.
- Cut or print out the articles, read them, and save them in the scrapbooks.
- Write a brief summary of what the articles say is happening to the animal.

Activity 61: Adding a Time Line

As students complete their scrapbooks, they could

- Create a time line to explain the progress of the animal and its situation, and
- Share their findings with the class.

Evaluation:

Students will be able to

- Identify news articles on an endangered species,
- Interpret the information,
- Track the progress of the animal, and
- Journal the process.

Related Resources:

Local newspapers
Regional and national newspapers via the Internet
Weekly newsmagazines such as Time and Newsweek
Internet news sources such as cnn.com and msnbc.com

Activities 62 and 63:
A is for African Elephant

Subjects: Life science, language arts, art
Grade levels: 1 and 2

> The class will create their own Endangered Animal Alphabet Book.

Preparation:

You will need

- Alphabet books such as *V is for Vanishing,* by Patricia Mullins, or any of Jerry Pallotta's alphabet books, including *The Dinosaur Alphabet Book, The Frog Alphabet Book, The Desert Animal Alphabet Book, The Extinct Alphabet Book,*
- Paper or large card stock, markers, crayons, paints, glue, pictures to cut and paste, information on endangered animals, and
- Materials to put the alphabet book together (binder, yarn, or metal rings).

Procedure:

- Examine *V Is for Vanishing*, an alphabet of endangered animals by Patricia Mullins. Using this as a model, have the class create their own picture book.
- Assign each student a letter of the alphabet and choose an endangered animal whose name begins with that letter.
- Create a sample page with the class, deciding what information should be on each page. This will vary according to grade level and ability. (See sample.)
- Have students create their pages and put all the pages together in a book.

Evaluation:

Students will successfully research an endangered animal, record their information artistically on a page, and create and arrange an alphabet book.

Related Print Resources:

Mullins, Patricia, *V Is for Vanishing, An Alphabet of Endangered Animals.* HarperCollins, 1993, 28 pp.

Pallotta, Jerry. *The Desert Alphabet Book*, Charlesbridge, 1994, unpaged.

_____. *The Dinosaur Alphabet Book.* Charlesbridge, 1991, unpaged.

_____. The Extinct Alphabet Book. Charlesbridge, 1993, unpaged.

_____. The Frog Alphabet Book. Charlesbridge, 1990, 32 pp.

A is for African elephant

Habitat: African savanna

Description:

Behavior:

Diet:

Reasons for Endangerment:

How Can We Help Them Survive?

Subjects: Life science, social studies
Grade levels: 1, 2, 3, 4, and 5

This begins a series of activities designed to inform students of what governments around the world are doing to assist in the recovery and preservation of endangered animals.

Preparation:

You will need

- Materials on endangered species,
- Copies of the Endangered Species Act of 1973, and
- Paper or whiteboard for recording ideas.

Procedure:

Ask students to

- Brainstorm and review reasons for population declines, including hunting, habitat loss, pollution, dietary needs, nesting needs, space and territory needs, slow growth and reproduction rate, natural limited population, and migration.
- Link reasons for endangerment to specific animals.

Evaluation:

Students will recognize causes endangering particular species of animals.

Related Internet Resources:

Kurpis, Lauren. *Causes for Endangerment.* ©1997—2000 Endangered Species.com. 5 October 2001. <http://www.endangeredspecie.com/causes_of_endangerment.htm>

Thinkquest. *Endangered Species of the Next Millennium.* © 1995-2001. 22 September 2001. <http://library.thinkquest.org/25014>

Activity 65:

Enemy Number One—Humans

Subjects: Life science, social studies

Grade levels: 1, 2, 3, 4, and 5

Students begin to understand how human activity threatens natural habitats and endangered species.

Preparation:

You will need

- Materials on endangered species,
- Copies of the Endangered Species Act of 1973,
- List of reasons various animals are endangered (from Activity 64), and
- Pictures of species that have become endangered because of human activity, such as the bald eagle, manatee, and box turtle.

Procedure:

Talk about examples of human activities and how they affect specific animals or plants; for example,

- Pollution—Effects on the bald eagle from DDT in the food chain,
- Over-hunting—African elephants are slaughtered for their valuable ivory tusks, and
- Over-collecting—People in other countries wanted box turtles for pets.

Evaluation:

Students will begin to realize how human activity has destroyed species populations.

Related Internet Resources:

Cornish, Jim. *Why Species Become Endangered. Gander Academy's Introduction to Endangered Species.* April 2000. 2 September 2001.
<http://www.stemnet.nf.ca/CITE/esreasons.htm>

SeaWorld. *Busch Gardens Animal Information Database.* ©2000 Busch Entertainment Corp. 2 September 2001.
<http://www.seaworld.org/infobooks/Endangered/esVI.html Endangered Species Profiles>

Hunted and Poached

Name of Animal	Hunted Part of Animal	Use of Animal Part

Hunted and Poached

Subjects: Life science, social studies
Grade levels: 3, 4, and 5

Students discuss hunting and poaching as causes of animal endangerment.

Preparation:

You will need

- A list of animals and reasons for endangerment from previous exercises,
- Materials on endangered animals, and
- Pictures or actual samples of ivory, fur, alligator skin, and so on.

Procedure:

- Let students examine samples or pictures of ivory, fur from an endangered animal, medicine powders from animal parts, and any other items that might illustrate the using of parts of poached animals.
- The class will begin recording animals and the reasons they are hunted and poached on a chart.
- Students, working in teams, select an animal and report on the ways hunting and poaching are threatening its survival. Reports will include posters with pictures of the animal and information on its habitat, behavior, size, weight, population, and family life.

Evaluation:

Students will understand how detrimental hunting and poaching can be.

Related Internet Resources:

Radley, Gary. *Animals of the World in Danger.* ©GR Software. 2 October 2001.
<http://www.animalsindanger.com/>

Kasnoff, Craig. *Bagheera in the Wild.* ©2001. 25 September 2001.
<http://www.bagheera.com/inthewild/>

San Diego Zoo. *Endangered Species.* ©2001 Zoological Society of San Diego. 25 September 2001.
<http://www.sandiegozoo.org/wildideas/animal/endangered.html>

Animal Populations Academy for Advancement of Science and Technology. *Animal Populations.*
©1996. 24 September 2001. <http://www.bergen.org/AAST/Projects/ES/AP/africa2.html>

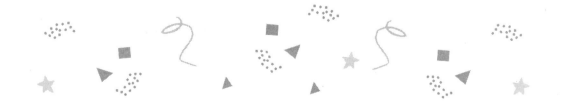

What Can We Do to Protect These Animals?

Name of Animal	Cause of Endangerment	Possible Protection

Activity 67:

The Endangered Species Act of 1973

Subjects: Life science, social studies, technology

Grade levels: 4 and 5

> Students begin to investigate our country's laws that protect endangered animals.

Preparation:

You will need

- List of animals and causes of endangerment from previous lesson,
- Copies of the What Can We Do To Protect These Animals? chart,
- Copy of The Endangered Species Act of 1973,
- Vocabulary journals,
- Dictionaries, and
- Internet access.

Procedure:

- Discuss with the class what might need to be done to protect endangered animals and what needs to be changed by legislation.
- Visit the U.S. Fish and Wildlife Service Web site at <http://endangered.fws.gov/index.html>.
- Browse this site for a preliminary understanding of the Endangered Species Act.
- Read the sections entitled
    - ▶ Species Information,
    - ▶ Endangered Species Act (as grade level permits), and
    - ▶ Endangered Species Glossary.
- Have students record words they do not know from the glossary.

Evaluation:

Students will gather background knowledge on the Endangered Species Act.

Related Internet Resources:

U.S. Fish & Wildlife Service. *The Endangered Species Program.* 27 September 2001. 11 October 2001.
<http://endangered.fws.gov/index.html>

Activitiy 68:

Diminishing Spaces

Subjects: Life science, geography
Grade levels: 1, 2, 3, 4, and 5

Students examine animals that are endangered because of habitat loss due to human activity.

Preparation:

You will need
- Materials on endangered animals and habitat loss and a
- World map or globe.

Procedure:

- Discuss habitat loss. The loss of a place to live, reproduce, and find food displaces many species and causes a decline in their numbers. Some animals that are endangered because of habitat loss:
- The Queen Alexandra birdwing butterfly
- Dwarf crocodile
- Indian and African elephants
- Komodo dragon
- Tigers
- Florida panther
- Manatee
- Grauer's gorilla
- As you discuss an animal, have students locate its habitat and decide what changes in the habitat have caused it to become endangered. Remind students that more than one thing can affect the animal population.

Activity 69:
Habitat Loss

Subjects: Life science, social studies

Grade levels: 4 and 5

Preparation:

You will need

- Materials on endangered animals and habitat loss,
- A world map or globe,
- Copies of the Habitat Loss Report Sheet (page 68), and
- Internet access.

Procedure:

Have students

- Choose one from the vast list of animals that are endangered due to habitat loss,
- Research the animal using print and nonprint resources, and
- Record their information on the Habitat Loss Report Sheet.

Evaluation:

Students will determine what happened to diminish a habitat. They will be able to research a specific animal that is endangered because of habitat loss, to describe it, and to list information about its habitat, behavior, life span, and endangered status.

Related Internet Resources:

Endangered Earth. *Bagheera in the Wild*. ©2000 ESBN. 22 September 2001.
<http://www.bagheera.com/inthewild/vanishing.htm>

Endangered Earth. *Bagheera in the Wild, Queen Alexandra Birdwing Butterfly*. ©2000 ESBN.
22 September 2001. <http://www.bagheera.com/inthewild/van_anim_buttrfly.htm>

Endangered Earth. *Bagheera in the Wild, Indian and African Elephants*. ©2000 ESBN.
22 September 2001. <http://www.bagheera.com/inthewild/van_anim_elephant.htm>

Endangered Earth. *Bagheera in the Wild, Dwarf Crocodile*. ©2000 ESBN. 22 September 2001.
dwarf crocodile - <http://www.bagheera.com/inthewild/van_anim_dwrfcroc.htm>

Komodo image from <http://www.animfactory.com/af_animals_reptiles_page_aa.html>
<http://dhr.dos.state.fl.us/symbols/animal.html> Florida panther
<http://www.kidsplanet.org/factsheets/florida_panther.html>

Habitat Loss Report Sheet

Name of Animal: _____

Description		Behavior	
Color:		Common activities:	
Average height:		Diet:	
Average weight:		Sleep habits:	
Unusual characteristics:		Family life:	
Habitat		**Lifespan/Endangered Status**	
Global location(s):		Natural enemies:	
Habitat:		Reasons for endangerment:	
Migration habits:		Number remaining:	

Pollution: Trip to a Wetland

Subjects: Life science, social studies, chemistry
Grade levels: 1, 2, 3, 4, and 5

Students examine another human activity that poses a serious threat to animals: water pollution and its effects on wildlife habitats.

Preparation:

■ Locate a wetland area that is close enough for a class field trip and arrange for transportation and additional adult supervision.

■ Include supplies for the trip such as
  ▶ Paper,
  ▶ Pencils,
  ▶ Clipboards,
  ▶ Disposal gloves, and
  ▶ Trash bags.

Procedure:

■ Divide the students in teams. Each team will assign a student the job of recorder to write down their findings. Be sure each team has responsible adult supervision. Each team will
  ▶ Look around the wetland area,
  ▶ Locate types and sources of pollution, and
  ▶ Record the types they identify.

■ After 10 minutes, have all groups meet at a designated spot and discuss what they have seen. Obvious pollution might include litter and other remnants of human activity. Emphasize that many kinds of pollution cannot be seen. Have the teams re-group to
  ▶ Collect the litter pollution,
  ▶ Put it in the trash bags (use disposable gloves for this), and
  ▶ Dispose of it in a dumpster.

Evaluation:

Students will be able to identify two or more pollutants in a bog, marsh, stream, or other local wetland area.

Activity 71:
Trashing Our Waters

Subject: Life science

Grade levels: 1, 2, 3, 4, and 5

Students learn how our waters become polluted.

Preparation:

Make a miniature lake resort for the classroom. You will need

- A dish pan,
- Plastic trees,
- A bridge,
- Other props for a pastoral water scene,
- White sugar,
- Clear vinegar,
- Potting soil,
- Small scraps of paper, and
- Brown food coloring.

Procedure:

- Discuss the wetland field trip (Activity 70), and the litter and pollution the students found. Present the miniature lake resort and ask them to imagine they are living in a cabin by a clean, rarely-frequented lake.
- There is no trash pickup. What happens to their trash? (Throw scraps of paper into the water.)
- They have a boat for transportation that uses fuel. (Throw some food coloring into the water.)
- They use fertilizer on their garden. (Throw white sugar into the water and let it dissolve.)
- They shower and use the toilet, and their wastewater goes into the lake. (Throw the vinegar and some potting soil into the water.)
- What has happened to the clear, clean water?

Evaluation:

Students will understand that pollution is often invisible.

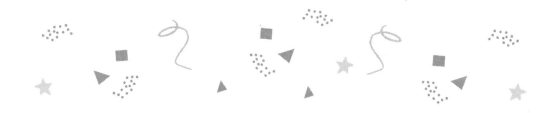

Pollution Poster

Subjects: Life science, social studies, chemistry, art
Grade levels: 1, 2, 3, 4, and 5

Students design a method to help people prevent water pollution and illustrate their idea with a poster.

Preparation:

You'll will need

- Poster board,
- Crayons or markers,
- Paste, and
- Other poster-making supplies.

Procedure:

- Review with the students the types of wetland pollution they saw and how people can prevent them.
- Record the answers on the board, and have students make posters visually explaining their pollution prevention ideas. Older students can also design and illustrate methods for waste disposal.
- Discuss and display the posters.

Evaluation:

Students will create posters that explain methods to prevent water pollution of a wetland.

Related Internet Resources:

O'Neill, Jim. DDT. ©University of New England. 1 November 2000. 1 October 2001. <http://www.ecoman.une.edu.au/Rsnr120/Mod3/lect32.html>

DDT, the Invisible Predator

Subject: Life science
Grade levels: 2, 3, 4, and 5

Students learn that chemicals like DDT can endanger animal species even though they cannot be seen.

Preparation:

Collect pictures of the bald eagle, California condor, whooping crane, and brown pelican.

Procedure:

Activity 73: Offer students a definition and explanation of the deadly hydrocarbons

■ Dichloro-diphenyl-trichloroethane (DDT) and

■ Polychlorinated biphenyls (PCBs), and

Their deadly effects:

■ DDT and PCBs become concentrated in food webs, strongly affecting species at the end of the food chain.

■ DDT and PCBs interfere with the calcium metabolism of birds, causing soft-shelled eggs and deformed young.

■ PCBs also impair reproduction in some carnivorous animals. Emphasize that these chemicals are invisible.

Activity 74: Who Suffers from DDT?
Display and discuss the photographs of the birds that have been driven almost to extinction by DDT.

Activity 75: Regulation for Regeneration.
Discuss the success of the regulations against DDT and the comeback of the Bald Eagle, our national symbol.

Evaluation:

Students will understand that clear water may still contain invisible pollutants that have a deadly effect on some species.

Related Internet Resources:

The American Museum of Natural History. *The American Peregrine Falcon.* ©1996. 22 September 2001. <http://www.amnh.org/nationalcenter/Endangered/falcon/falcon.html>

Lyon, Lynda. *Endangered Species Pesticide Issues.* ©2001 About.com, Inc. 22 September 2001. <http://environment.about.com/library/weekly/bles15.htm>

National Park Service, United States Department of the Interior. *Rare Threatened and Endangered Plants.* ©1996 nature.nps.gov. 22 September 2001. <http://www.nature.nps.gov/pubs/i&mann96/07-09.htm>

Thinkquest Library of Entries. *Save Our Earth and Make a Difference.* ©1995—2001 Thinkquest, Inc. 22 September 2001. <http://library.thinkquest.org/2988/e-animals.htm#>

U.S. Fish & Wildlife Service. *Fish and Wildlife Species; Peregrine Falcon.* ©2001 USFWS. 22 September 2001. <http://species.fws.gov/bio_pere.html>

Activity 76:

The Bald Eagle, a Success Story

Subjects: Life science, social studies
Grade levels: 1, 2, 3, 4, and 5

Students learn about the successful preservation of the bald eagle.

Preparation:

Bald eagle time line:

- Declared the United States' national symbol in 1782.

- 1918 Migratory Bird Treaty Act prohibits taking, selling and transporting migratory birds.

- The Bald Eagle Protection Act of 1940 prohibits taking, possessing, and selling bald eagles.

- The Endangered Species Preservation Act of 1966 included the bald eagle.

- On February 14, 1978, the bald eagle was listed under the Endangered Species Act as threatened in Michigan, Minnesota, Oregon, Washington, and Wisconsin and endangered in the remaining 43 coterminous states.

- In July 1995, the U.S. Fish and Wildlife Service downlisted the species to threatened throughout the lower 48 states.

Procedure:

- Using the bald eagle KWL chart on page 75, encourage students to

- Ask and answer questions about the bald eagle.

- Complete research, and

- Fill out a Bald Eagle Fact Sheet (page 74).

- Display the completed fact sheets.

Evaluation:

Students will understand how enforced legislation can make a difference.

Related Internet Resources:

"The Bald Eagle." *American Bald Eagle Information.* ©2001 baldeagleinfo.com 23 September 2001. <http://www.baldeagleinfo.com/>

U.S. Fish & Wildlife Service. *The Bald Eagle.* Last modified October 12, 2000. 23 September 2001. <http://endangered.fws.gov/i/b0h.html>

Bald Eagle Fact Sheet

Name: _____

List ten facts about the Bald Eagle:

_____

_____

_____

_____

_____

_____

_____

_____

_____

_____

_____

_____

_____

_____

_____

_____

_____

_____

_____

_____

Include information on: habitat, the scientific name, predator, some physical characteristics, dietary habits, and the symbolism of the Bald Eagle.

KWL Chart

What I know:

_____

_____

_____

_____

What I want to learn:

_____

_____

_____

_____

What I learned:

_____

_____

_____

_____

Your State's Endangered Animals

Subjects: Life science, geography, technology

Grade levels: 3, 4, and 5

Students locate lists of endangered animals in their own state.

Preparation:

For this activity, you will need Internet connection, and paper and writing tools to record findings.

Procedure:

■ On the Internet, go to either of these pages:

▶ EE-Link Endangered Species state and region page
<http://eelink.net/EndSpp/organizations-stateandregional.html>. Select your region, which will direct you to the Fish and Wildlife page, where you can select your state.

▶ U.S. Fish and Wildlife Service Threatened and Endangered Species System
<http://ecos.fws.gov/Webpage/>. Select
- State Lists (USA),
- Your state,
- Animal for which you want information and statistics, and
- "Learn More About This Species."

■ Have students record their findings, using the Endangered Animals in My State chart (page 79). If there are many endangered animals in your state, assign a different one to each student, or have them work in teams.

Evaluation:

Students will locate information about their state's endangered animals.

Related Internet Resources:

EE–Link Endangered Species Page ©1996—1999
<http://eelink.net/EndSpp/organizations-stateandregional.html>

U.S. Fish and Wildlife Service Threatened and Endangered Species System (TESS)
<http://ecos.fws.gov/Webpage/>

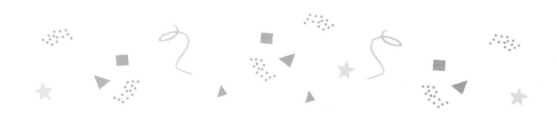

Activity 78:
Up Close and Endangered

Subjects: Life science, geography

Grade levels: 3, 4, and 5

Report on a specific endangered animal of the region or state.

Preparation:

This activity is based on information gathered in Activity 77.

Procedure:

Have students discuss

■ The variety of animals in their region,

■ Names of animals they located,

■ If they have seen one of these endangered animals,

■ If they knew it was endangered,

■ What they think they can do to help support the species, and

■ What is already being done on a local level to support the species.

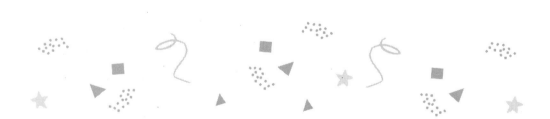

Investigating Local Endangered Animals

Subjects: Life science, geography

Grade levels: 3, 4, and 5

This is an extension of Activities 77 and 78.

Procedure:

■ Assign each student a specific local animal to investigate further and answer the above discussion questions.

■ Encourage students to use both print and digital sources of information.

Evaluation:

Students will become aware that endangered animals can be a local concern.

Endangered Animals In My State

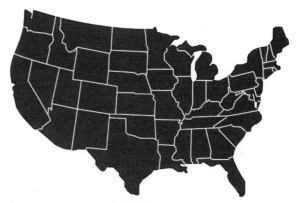

Directions: Locate your state or region on the map. Label and color it. From your previous research, list the endangered animals in your state or region.

Name of Animal

Local Endangered Animals

What is the name of the animal?

_____

Have you ever seen one of these endangered animals? _____

Did you know it was endangered? _____

What can you do to help support the species? _____

Do they live near you?_____

What is already being done on a local level to support the species?

_____

_____

_____

_____

Facts about your animal:

1. _____

2. _____

3. _____

Activities 81, 82, 83, and 84:

Regional Animal Slide Show

Subjects: Life science, geography, technology
Grade levels: 4 and 5

Students create a six-slide presentation about a local endangered animal.

Preparation:

Facts acquired from previous activity assignment.

Procedure:

Activity 81: Have students create a storyboard for their slide show using index cards.

Activity 82: Make the first two slides.
- Slide One—Title of slide show and name of student
- Slide Two—Name and picture of animal and reason for endangerment

Activity 83: Make slides three and four.
- Map displaying the local habitat or a verbal description of the area and habitat
- Information specific to the animal

Activity 84: Research local groups and legislation as background for slides five and six.
- Legislation or groups supporting the animal
- Credits, including bibliography with Web sites

Evaluation:

Students will demonstrate their ability to extract information about a local endangered animal and compile the information into a slide presentation.

Endangered Species Trading Cards

Subjects: Life science, art

Grade levels: 1, 2, 3, 4, and 5

Students create sets of Endangered Species Trading Cards.

Preparation:

You will need card stock cut into standard baseball card size: 2-1/2" by 3-1/2".

Procedure:

Activity 85: Reproduce templates (page 83) and have students create cards. They should draw a picture of the animal in the box and fill in the other information. Encourage duplicates to enable trading.

Activity 86: Let the students play and trade their cards. Have them tell if any of the animals are a danger to each other or to each others' habitats.

Evaluation:

Students will demonstrate knowledge of endangered animals and enjoy a trading game.

Name of Animal

_____

Habitat _____

Diet_____

Behavior_____

Reasons endangered

_____

_____

Name of Animal

_____

Habitat _____

Diet_____

Behavior_____

Reasons endangered

_____

_____

Name of Animal

_____

Habitat _____

Diet_____

Behavior_____

Reasons endangered

_____

_____

Name of Animal

_____

Habitat _____

Diet_____

Behavior_____

Reasons endangered

_____

_____

Flashcards

Subjects: Life science, technology
Grade levels: 1, 2, 3, 4, and 5

> Follow these directions and suggestions for creating flashcards about endangered animals. Use sample sets or make your own. Students can help create sets for the class as well.

Preparation:

- Make up sets of questions and answers or select a topic and ask students to brainstorm questions and answers.
- You'll need 3 inch by 5 inch index cards or card stock.

Procedure:

In a word processing program

- Create a table.
- Adjust the table settings to 3 rows and 1 column.
- Select the Table Properties; set the column width to 5 inches and row height to 2.75 inches.
- Select a font you like. The sample template is created with Comic Sans MS with a font size of 28 because it fits the card nicely.
- Type the questions. Use the same table format for each page.
- Run the set of questions through the printer.
- Repeat the process for the answer cards. You can either run the same cards through the printer, printing on the reverse side, or print another set and paste them onto the other side of the index cards.
- You can also visit The Flashcard Exchange at <http://www.flashcardexchange.com/index.jsp\> and set up an account (it's free) to make flashcard sets.

Evaluation:

Students will demonstrate their knowledge of endangered species and their ability to create a table in a word processing program.

Related Internet Resources:

The Flashcard Exchange ©2001 Flashcard Exchange.
<http://www.flashcardexchange.com/index.jsp\>

Habitat Flashcards

Note: Activities 88—91 are extensions of Activity 87.

Grade levels: 3, 4 and 5

Procedure:

Use these clues to make sets of flashcards on habitats:

■ A windy, partly dry sea of grass with few trees (Grassland)

■ Cool, treeless, and dry (Tundra)

■ Very dry, either hot or cold (Desert)

■ Warm and very wet (Tropical rainforest)

■ Teeming with plants and animals that live in the water, above the water, and in the surrounding area (Pond)

■ Very cold, windy, often snowy, located around the North Pole (Arctic)

■ Warm, clear, shallow, rich in life, and within the ocean habitat (Coral reefs)

■ Covers three-fourths of the earth's surface and contains roughly 97 percent of the earth's water supply (Ocean)

■ An elevated land form that contains extensive and varied climatic conditions, vegetation, wildlife, and human cultural diversity (Mountains)

Evaluation:

Students will demonstrate knowledge of the characteristics of habitats.

Activity 89:
Classification Flashcards

Procedure:

Use these clues to make sets of flashcards on species classification:

- Cold-blooded, breathes through gills, lives in water and lays eggs (Fish)
- Warm-blooded, has feathers and wings, lays eggs; most individuals can fly (Bird)
- Invertebrates that are soft-bodied animals that live in hard shells (Mollusks)
- Cold-blooded, lives both on land, breathing with lungs, and in water, breathing through gills (Amphibian)
- Cold-blooded, breathes with lungs, has scales, and lays eggs (Reptiles)
- Warm-blooded, nourished by their mother's milk, most are born live (Mammals)
- Animals with backbones (Vertebrates)
- Mammals whose females carry their young in an external pouch (Marsupials)
- Animals who eat only plants (Herbivores)
- Humans and their closest mammalian relatives, with flexible arms and legs, skilled fingers, and big brains (Primates)

Evaluation:

Students will demonstrate an understanding of animal classification and identify the class to which an animal belongs.

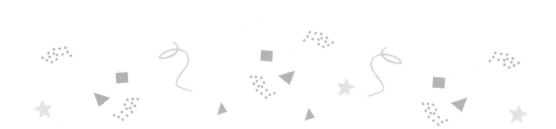

Endangered Animal Flashcards

Procedure:

Use these clues to make sets of flashcards on endangered animals:

■ Biggest land animal; only natural enemy is man (Elephant)

■ The heaviest animal living in the North American grasslands; an herbivore that appears in Native American folklore (Bison)

■ A long-tailed, fierce wildcat that lives deep in deciduous forests, rain forests, grasslands, and deserts of North and South America (Cougar, panther, puma, mountain lion)

■ Biggest lizard in the world and a fierce predator (Komodo dragon)

■ Gentle, slow-moving sea mammal that lives in coastal waters and canals (Manatee)

■ Black and white mammal that eats only bamboo; lives in China (Panda)

■ A baleen whale that is a bottom feeder, migrates long distances, and lives in small pods (Gray whale)

■ Shy, peaceful herbivore primate that lives in western Africa (Gorilla)

■ Black and white fast-running mammal that lives on African savannas (Zebra)

■ A large reptile that lives in freshwater, slow-moving rivers, swamps, marshes, and lakes from southern Virginia coast to the Rio Grande in Texas; was hunted for its hide (American alligator)

Evaluation:

Students will be able to identify endangered animals from descriptions of their characteristics and habitats.

Activity 91:
Causes for Endangerment Flashcards

Procedure:

Use these clues to make sets of flashcards on reasons species have become endangered:

■ Asian otter: freshwater wetlands and swamp (Destruction of the otter's wetland habitat)

■ Siberian tiger: large cat with thick yellow fur and dark stripes (Hunted for its skin)

■ Giant panda: a large mammal with dramatic black-and-white pattern coloration to its fur. It has black markings on the ears, limbs, shoulders, and around the eyes. (Loss of habitat)

■ Snow leopard: lives in the mountains of central Asia; beautiful coat of pale gray fur with black rosettes and small spots, and a black streak along the spine; mainly nocturnal; usually two to three cubs in a litter (Over-hunted for its fur)

■ California condor: one of the largest flying birds in the world; can soar and glide for hours without beating its wings; searches from the air for dead animals, like deer or cattle; feeds only on carrion (dead animals) (Lead pollution of their food sources; shooting and collisions with manmade objects)

■ Grizzly (brown) bear: lives in mountain forests, open meadows, and large river valleys (Historically hunting, but presently loss of wilderness due to human use for recreation)

■ Manatee: waters of southern Florida peninsula; large gray or brown aquatic mammal without hind limbs. Forelimbs are modified as flippers; tails are flattened horizontally and rounded. Manatees will consume any aquatic vegetation available to them and sometimes even shoreline vegetation. (Initial population decreases from over-harvesting for meat, oil, and leather. Today, accidental collisions with watercraft are a major cause for endangerment.

■ Bald eagle: a large raptor with a white head and tail and a dark brown body. Our national symbol (Food contaminated by DDT used to control mosquitoes caused their eggshells to be thin and easily broken in the nest.)

■ Bottlenose dolphin: live in temperate and tropical oceans (Caught in fishermen's nets)

■ Polar bear: the largest bear, found around the Arctic sea ice and across the polar basin (Excessive hunting)

Evaluation:

Students will demonstrate knowledge of reasons animals have become endangered.

COOL, TREELESS, AND DRY

VERY DRY, EITHER HOT OR COLD

TEEMING WITH PLANT AND ANIMALS THAT LIVE IN THE WATER, ABOVE THE WATER, AND IN THE AREA SURROUNDING

TUNDRA

DESERT

POND

The Same but Different: Animal Comparisons

Subjects: Life science, critical thinking

Grade levels: 3, 4, and 5

> Many animals have the same general name, but are very different. They live in different habitats, have different characteristics and needs, and look different. These activities give students an opportunity to investigate some of these similarities and differences.

Preparation:

You will need

- Information on endangered species,
- Print resources,
- Magazines and pictures students can use to cut and paste, and
- Internet access.

Procedure:

- Brainstorm endangered animals that have similar names. Assign or have students
  - ▶ Select or be assigned a pair or group of endangered animals and
  - ▶ Create a comparison chart or Venn diagram for each set of endangered animals.
- Display the charts.

Activity 93: Asian Elephant and African Elephant

- All About Mammals. *African Elephant*. ©Enchanted Learning.com. 9 September 2001. <http://www.enchantedlearning.com/subjects/mammals/elephant/Africancoloring.shtml>
- All About Mammals. *Asian Elephant*. ©Enchanted Learning.com. 9 September 2001. <http://www.enchantedlearning.com/subjects/mammals/elephant/Asiancoloring.shtml>

Activity 94: Tigers

Siberian Tiger

- All About Mammals. *Siberian Tiger*. ©Enchanted Learning.com. 9 September 2001. <http://www.enchantedlearning.com/subjects/mammals/tiger/Siberiatigerprintout.shtml>
- Annabell, Maxine. Tiger Territory. *Armur*. ©2001. 9 September 2001. http://www.lairWeb.org.nz/tiger/amur.html

Bengal Tiger

- All About Mammals. *Bengal Tiger*. Enchanted Learning.com. 9 September 2001. <http://www.enchantedlearning.com/subjects/mammals/tiger/Bengaltigerprintout.shtml>
- Annabell, Maxine. Tiger Territory. *Bengal*. ©2001. 9 September 2001. <http://www.lairWeb.org.nz/tiger/bengal.html>

Sumatran Tiger

- 5 Tigers. The Tiger Information Center. *Sumatran Tigers*. ©1995—2001 Tiger Information Center. 9 September 2001. <http://www.5tigers.org/Basics/Subsp_distribution/sumatran.htm>

- Annabell, Maxine. Tiger Territory. *Sumatran*. ©2001. 9 September 2001. <http://www.lairWeb.org.nz/tiger/sumatran.html>

Indochinese Tiger

- 5 Tigers. The Tiger Information Center. *Indochinese Tigers*. ©1995—2001 Tiger Information Center. 9 September 2001. <http://www.5tigers.org/Basics/Subsp_distribution/ichinese.htm>

- Annabell, Maxine. Tiger Territory. *Corbetts*. ©2001. 9 September 2001. http://www.lairWeb.org.nz/tiger/corbetts.html

South China Tiger

- 5 Tigers. The Tiger Information Center. *South China Tigers*. ©1995—2001 Tiger Information Center. 9 September 2001. <http://www.5tigers.org/Basics/Subsp_distribution/sochina.htm>

- Annabell, Maxine. Tiger Territory. *South Chinese*. ©2001. 9 September 2001. <http://www.lairWeb.org.nz/tiger/southchinese.html>

Activity 95: Whales

Blue Whales

- All About Mammals. *Blue Whale*. ©Enchanted Learning.com. 9 September 2001. <http://www.enchantedlearning.com/subjects/whales/activities/whaletemplates/ Bluetemplate.shtml>

- American Cetacean Society. *American Cetacean Society Fact Sheet*. Blue Whales. Updated 26 January 2001. 8 September 2001. <http://www.acsonline.org/factpack/bluewhl.htm>

Gray Whales

- All About Mammals. *Gray Whale*. ©Enchanted Learning.com. 9 September 2001. <http://www.enchantedlearning.com/subjects/whales/activities/whaletemplates/ Graytemplate.shtml>

- Kasnoff, Craig. *In the Wild. Oceans. Gray Whale*. ©1996. 9 September 2001. <http://www.bagheera.com/inthewild/van_anim_grywhale.htm>

Humpback Whale

- All About Mammals. *Humpback Whale*. ©Enchanted Learning.com. 9 September 2001. <http://www.enchantedlearning.com/subjects/whales/activities/whaletemplates/ Humptemplate.shtml>

- U.S. Department of Commerce. *Detailed Information About Humpback Whales*. ©2001 Laura Drumm. 9 September 2001. <http://nmml.afsc.noaa.gov/education/cetaceans/humpback2.htm>

Activity 96: Pandas

Giant Pandas

- All About Mammals. *Giant Pandas*. ©Enchanted Learning.com. 9 September 2001. <http://www.enchantedlearning.com/ subjects/mammals/panda/Color.shtml/>

- Mosbacker, Linda. *Endangered Animals, Pandas*. ©UEN. 7 September 2001. <http://www.uen.org/utahlink/activities/view_activity.cgi?activity_id=3814>

- World Wildlife Fund Endangered Species. *Pandas*. ©World Wildlife Fund. 20 August 2001. <http://www.worldwildlife.org/pandas/>

Red Pandas

- Animal Magazine. *Red Pandas*. ©2000—2001 Nature.com. 4 September 2001. <http://www.animal-information.com/text/red-panda.html>

■ Massicot, Paul. Last modified 29 July 2001; ©2001 Animal Info. 4 September 2001.
<http://www.animalinfo.org/species/carnivor/ailufulg.htm>

Activity 97: Wolves

Red Wolves

■ The Wild Ones Animal Index. *Red Wolves.* ©2000 The Wild Ones. 9 October 2001.
<http://www.thewildones.org/Animals/redWolf.html>

■ U.S. Fish and Wildlife Service. *Red wolf, (Canis rufus).* ©2001 USFWS. 9 October 2001.
<http://species.fws.gov/bio_rwol.html>

Gray Wolves

■ Enchanted Learning.com. *Animal Printouts; The Gray Wolf.* ©1999—2001. 9 October 2001.
<http://www.enchantedlearning.com/subjects/mammals/dog/Graywolfprintout.shtml>

■ Williams, Lezle. *Gray Wolves, (Canis lupus).* ©2000 The Wild Ones. 9 October 2001.
<http://www.thewildones.org/Animals/grayWolf.html>

Activity 98: Rhinoceros

Black Rhinoceros

■ The International Rhinoceros Foundation. *Black Rhinoceros.* ©2000. 9 October 2001.
<http://www.rhinos-irf.org/rhinos/black.html>

■ In the Wild: Africa. *The Black Rhinoceros.* ©2000 ESBN. 9 October 2001.
<http://www.bagheera.com/inthewild/vanishing.htm>

Javan Rhinoceros

■ The International Rhinoceros Foundation. *Black Rhinoceros.* ©2000. 9 October 2001.
<http://www.rhinos-irf.org/rhinos/javan.html>

■ World Wildlife Fund. *Javan Rhinoceros.* ©2001 WWF. 9 October 2001.
<http://www.panda.org/resources/publications/species/threatened/JavanRhinoceros/>

Sumatran Rhino

■ The International Rhinoceros Foundation. *Sumatran Rhinoceros.* ©2000. 9 October 2001.
<http://www.rhinos-irf.org/rhinos/sumatran.html>

■ Massicot, Paul. *Animal Info–Sumatran Rhinoceros.* ©2001 Animal Info. 9 October 2001.
<http://www.animalinfo.org/species/artiperi/dicesuma.htm>

There are many more species to compare and contrast.

Evaluation:

Students will identify similarities and differences between species with similar names.

Who Named You? Unusual Species

Subjects: Life science, technology
Grade levels: 2, 3, 4, and 5

Although their plight is a sad one, many endangered species have humorous names. These activities explore some of them.

Preparation:

For this activity you will need either print materials or Internet connection.

Procedure:

Have students

■ Look up the origin of the name,

■ Get information about these endangered animals, and

■ Tell where they have heard the name used before, when it was not associated with an endangered animal.

Activity 99: Zorro: A dog-like fox from South America

■ All About Mammals. *Small-Eared Zorro*. ©Enchanted Learning.com. 6 September 2001.
<http://www.enchantedlearning.com/subjects/mammals/fox/Smallearedzorro.shtml>

■ The IUCN/SSC Canid Specialist Group's Canid Species Accounts. *Small Eared Zorro*. Updated 2 February 2001. 6 September 2001.
<http://www.enchantedlearning.com/subjects/mammals/fox/Smallearedzorro.shtml>

Activity 100: Tasmanian Devil

■ All About Mammals. *Tasmanian Devil*. ©Enchanted Learning.com. 6 September 2001.
<http://www.enchantedlearning.com/subjects/mammals/marsupial/Tazdevilprintout.shtml>

■ Unique Australian Animals. *Tasmanian Devil*. ©Australian Ring. 6 September 2001.
<http://home.mira.net/~areadman/devil.htm>

Activity 101: Sloth

■ American Zoo & Aquarium Association Bear Advisory Group Sloth Bear. Last update 12 April 1999. 26 August 2001. http://www.bearden.org/slobear.html

■ Kalasinskas, Ron. *Two-toed Sloth*. ©1999—2001 Animals of the Rainforest. 26 August 2001.
<http://www.animalsoftherainforest.com/sloth.htm>

Activity 102: Numbat

■ Kasnoff, Craig. *In the Wild: Australia. Numbat*. ©2000 ESBN. 26 August 2001.
<http://www.bagheera.com/inthewild/van_anim_numbat.htm>

■ University of Michigan Museum of Zoology. M*yrmecobius fasciatus Numbat*. ©1995—2001, The Regents of the University of Michigan. 26 August 2001.
<http://animaldiversity.ummz.umich.edu/accounts/myrmecobius/m._fasciatus$narrative.html>

Activity 103: Jackass Penguin

- ■ Wildchannel.com. *The Jackass Penguin.* ©2000, 2001. Steel Spyda Ltd. 26 August 2001. <http://www.wildchannel.com/features/jackass1.htm>
- ■ All About Mammals. *Jackass Penguin.* ©Enchanted Learning.com. 26 August 2001. <http://www.enchantedlearning.com/subjects/birds/printouts/Jackasspenguin.shtml>

Evaluation:

Students will recognize familiar names they may not have previously associated with endangered animals.

Saving Endangered Species

Subjects: Life science, social studies, language arts
Grade levels: 1, 2, 3, 4, and 5

Students find ways to help endangered animals, acting either as a group or individually.

Preparation:

You will need
- Internet access,
- Lists of local environmental organizations
- Writing paper, and
- Envelopes.

Procedure:

Guide students in a search for information—via Internet, pamphlets, or other print materials—on how they can help endangered animals through local organizations. As a group, they can decide what they want to do. They may prefer to act as a group or to make individual efforts.

Activity 104: Support the Endangered Species Act

Write to the
U.S. Fish and Wildlife Service
Division of Endangered Species
4401 N. Fairfax Drive, Room 420
Arlington, VA 22203

Help students write letters expressing their support for protection of these species and their habitats. Encourage them to speak out in favor of the Endangered Species Act.

Related Internet Resources:

U.S. Fish and Wildlife Service. *Endangered Species Program.* Last updated 27 September 2001. 3 October 2001. <http://endangered.fws.gov/>

Activity 105: Contact a Local Nature Organization

Have students contact a local nature organization and ask how they can become involved in saving wildlife.

Related Internet Resources:

U.S. Fish and Wildlife Service. *How Can Kids Help?* ©U.S. Fish and Wildlife Service. <http://endangered.fws.gov/kids/how_help.htm>

Activity 106: Wildlife Rehabilitation Center

Contact a wildlife rehabilitation center in your area and find out what educational programs or activities it offers to the public. Send home this information in a classroom newsletter.

Related Internet Resources:

U.S. Fish & Wildlife Service. *Refuges.* 5 October 2001. <http://refuges.fws.gov/>

Outdoors 411 Outdoors Information Directory. *Wildlife Rehabilitation Centers in the U.S.* ©1998—2000 Southeastern Outdoors. 5 October 2001. <http://www.southeasternoutdoors.com/rehab_usa.html>

Activity 107: We're Going to the Zoo

Take the class on a field trip to a zoo and ask students to answer these questions:

- Are any of the animals you see endangered?
- Are they being bred in captivity?
- Is this environment suitable for their species?
- What can you do to help them survive?

Evaluation:

Students will take an active role in saving endangered animals.

Ames, Lee J., *Draw 50 Endangered Animals*. Doubleday, 1993, unpaged.
Ames gives step-by-step directions on how to draw different types of endangered animals.

Behm, Barbara J. and Jean-Christopher Balouet. *Endangered Wildlife, In Peril.* Gareth Stevens, 1994, 32 pp.
An overview of the number and types of animal species that are endangered throughout the world. It focuses on the reasons for species becoming endangered.

_____, *Endangered Animals of the Northern Continents.* Gareth Stevens, 1994, 32 pp.
Detailed investigation of a cross-section of endangered animal species in Europe, Asia and North America.

Burn, Barbara, *North American Mammals*. Bonanza Books, 1984, 94 pp.
Pictures and text on the mammals of North America, both endangered and nonendangered.

Burton, Bob, *Endangered Birds!* Gareth Stevens, 1996, 64 pp.
Burton defines the endangered bird species from all parts of the world with color photographs and habitat maps for each species.

_____, *Endangered Environments!* Gareth Stevens, 1996, 64 pp.
This title explores the animals' environments and explains why we need to protect nature's treasures for future generations.

_____, *Endangered Mammals!* Gareth Stevens, 1996. 64 pp.
Part of the Endangered! series, this book looks at some of the most at-risk mammals and explains why they are endangered and what is being done to preserve them.

_____, *Endangered Sea Life!* Gareth Stevens, 1995, 64 pp.
Part of the Endangered! series, this book looks at some of the most at-risk marine species and explains why they are endangered and what is being done to preserve them.

Coleman, Graham, *The Extinct Species Collection: Passenger Pigeon.*
Gareth Stevens, 1996, 24 pp.
Coleman tells the story of the extinction of the passenger pigeon, once thought to be the most plentiful bird in the world. In 1860, scientists estimated that there were between five and 10 billion in existence. Only 54 years later, the last one died in captivity.

Davis, Jodie, *Easy-to-Make Endangered Species to Stitch & Stuff.*
Williamsburg Publishing, 1992, 187 pp.
Jodie Davis guides the creation of hand-crafted endangered species projects. These crafts are too advanced for K-5 students but can be done in preparation for a class activity by a parent or teacher.

Facklam, Margery, *And Then There Was One*. Little, Brown, 1990. 56 pp.
This book examines the reasons animals disappear from Earth. Pencil drawings by Pamela Johnson add to the informative text.

Few, Robert, *Macmillan's Children's Guide to Endangered Animals.*
Macmillan, 1993, 96 pp.
This guide lists over 150 endangered animals, explaining how their survival is threatened and what is being done to protect their shrinking populations. Maps show distribution, population size, and conservation status of a wide selection of animals. The information is organized by geographic location.

Fleisher, Paul, *Gorillas.* Benchmark Books, 2001, 112 pp.
This book briefly explains scientific classification. Fleisher discusses animals' physical and behavioral characteristics, relationships with humans, and their places in mythology and throughout history.

Galan, Mark, *There's Still Time.* National Geographic Society, 1997, 40 pp.
A beautifully photographed, well documented book that celebrates the successes of the Endangered Species Act of 1974.

George, Michael, *Wolves.* Child's World, 2000, 32 pp.
This beautiful book dispels the myth that wolves are man's enemies. It explains that the red wolf is endangered, but most of the other wolf family members are not.

Gouck, Maura, *Mountain Lions.* Child's World, 2001, 32 pp.
This book discusses the characteristics, behavior, and habitat of the endangered mountain lion.

Grimbly, Shona, *Cheetahs.* Benchmark, 1999, 32 pp.
Once ranging over much of Africa, the Near East and northern India, cheetahs survive today only in small areas of Africa and Iran. This book explores why they are endangered and what we can do to save them from extinction.

Hall, Derek, *Baby Animals.* Candlewick, 1992, 61 pp.
This re-issue of a book first published in 1984 simply relates the stories of the daily lives of five baby animal species that are endangered: elephant, tiger, panda, polar bear, and gorilla. The illustrations are lovely.

Lantier, Patricia and Feeney, Kathy, *The Wonder of Pandas.* Gareth Stevens, 2001, 48 pp.
With this book's vivid color photos and clear explanations, a child can enter the world of the panda and understand its habits and habitat.

Lessem, Don, *Dinosaurs to Dodos: An Encyclopedia of Extinct Animals.* Scholastic, 1999, 112pp.
Lessem tells the story of the creatures that once lived on our plant and have now disappeared, never to return. Major extinction events are discussed in sequence.

Markert, Jenny, *Elephants,* Child's World, 2001, 32 pp.
Clear text and beautiful photographs inform readers about the lives of both African and Asian elephants.

Print Resources

_____, *Tigers*. Child's World, 1998, 32 pp.
Beautiful photographs and explicit text explain the life of tigers and their relationship to other animals and man.

Markert, Jenny, *Zebras*. Child's World, 2001, 32 pp.
Is the zebra white with black stripes or black with white stripes? This book explores the mysteries of the zebra, its habitat and threats.

Maynard, Thane, *Komodo Dragons*. Child's World, 1997, 32 pp.
Maynard describes the beauty and mystery of the endangered Komodo dragon, the biggest lizard in the world.

McDonald, Mary Ann. *Leopards*. Child's World, 1999, 32 pp.
With stunning photographs and clear text, this book explains the life of a leopard, its solitary existence, and its need for protection.

_____, *Manatees*. Child's World, 1998, 32 pp.
From the sailors' mystery mermaid to today's peaceful grazer, this book explains the life and physiology of the manatee, now endangered because of man's inconsiderate treatment of its habitats.

Merrick, Patrick, *Snow Leopards*. Child's Press, 1998, 32 pp.
The snow leopard, a beautiful member of the cat family, lives high in the mountains of Asia. Its only natural enemy is man. This book explains its plight and hope for survival.

Mullins, Patricia, *V for Vanishing: An Alphabet of Endangered Animals*.
HarperCollins, 1993, 28 pp.
Collage illustrations of endangered species portray their beauty and fragile existence.

Murray, Peter, *Rhinos*. Child's World, 2001, 32 pp.
A simplified but informative look at rhinos and their causes of endangerment.

National Geographic Society, *Animals in Danger, Trying to Save Our Wildlife*. National Geographic Society, 1978, 32 pp.
Brief text and pictures describe the habits and behaviors of a variety of endangered animals.

Pallotta, Jerry. *The Extinct Alphabet Book*. Charlesbridge, 1993, unpaged.
This alphabet of extinct creatures includes mammals, fish, birds, and insects.

_____, *The Frog Alphabet Book*. Charlesbridge, 1990, 32 pp.
The alphabet introduces a variety of frogs and other amphibians.

_____, *The Desert Alphabet Book*. Charlesbridge, 1994, unpaged.
An alphabet book of desert life.

_____, *The Dinosaur Alphabet Book*. Charlesbridge, 1991, unpaged.
Full of interesting facts, this alphabet book introduces children to the fascinating world of dinosaurs.

Print Resources

Patton, Don, *Sea Turtles*. Child's World, 1996, 32 pp.
This book, complete with extraordinary photographs of sea turtles, clearly explains the variety of sea turtles, their migration and habits, and their current endangered situation.

Rutten, Joshua, *Red Pandas*, Child's World, 1998, 32 pp.
A combination of stunning photography and simple text, this book explains the essential differences between giant pandas and red pandas. Both are endangered.

Silverstein, Alvin, *The Manatee*. Millbrook, 1995. 64 pp.
Silverstein tracks the manatee's history and habitats and the dangers it faces as well as efforts to save the species.

Stotsky, Sandra, *Endangered Species, Wild and Rare*. Chelsea House, 1998, 83 pp.
An award-winning book filled with arts and crafts, literature activities, hands-on science activities, and lots more, designed to teach children about endangered species and how human beings can help prevent further extinction.

Thapar, Valmik, *Tiger*. Raintree Steck-Vaughn, 2000, 48 pp.
Thapar follows the life of a Bengal tiger through the forests of India.

Vergoth, Harin and Lampton, Christopher, *Endangered Species*.
Franklin Watts, 1988, 111 pp.
The authors explain the diminishing diversity of species in our world.

Woods, Theresa, *Jaguars*. Child's World, 2001, 32 pp.
This book beautifully illustrates the majestic jaguar, endangered by man's encroaching on its natural habitats.

Wright, Alexandra, *Will We Miss Them?* Charlesbridge, 1992, unpaged.
An engaging introduction to the lives of endangered species from the perspective of an 11-year-old author.

❖ Index ❖

❖ Index ❖